POCKET FACTFILES

Endangered
Animals

Project Director: **Graham Bateman**
Managing Editor: **Shaun Barrington**
Picture Manager: **Claire Turner**
Production: **Clive Sparling**
Design & Editorial: **Kinsey & Harrison**
  Designer: **Edward Kinsey**
  Editors: **James Harrison,**
         Louisa Somerville
  Index: **Patricia Hymans**

Produced by
Andromeda Oxford Limited,
11–13 The Vineyard, Abingdon,
Oxfordshire OX14 3PX
www.andromeda.co.uk
© copyright Andromeda Oxford Ltd 2003

Library of Congress Cataloging-in-
Publication Data Available

10 9 8 7 6 5 4 3 2 1

Published in 2003 by Sterling Publishing
Co., Inc.
387 Park Avenue South,
New York, NY 10016
Distributed in Canada by Sterling
Publishing,
c/o Manda Group,
One Atlantic Avenue, Suite 105
Toronto, Ontario, Canada M6K 3E7

Printed in Hong Kong

Sterling ISBN 1-4027-0292-2

Picture Credits

Abbreviations
BCC   Bruce Coleman Collection
NHPA   Natural History Photographic Agency
OSF   Oxford Scientific Films

7l Robin Bush/OSF; 7r Hilton-Taylor, C. (Compiler)
(2000). 2000 IUCN Red List of Threatened Species.
IUCN, Gland, Switzerland and Cambridge, UK. xviii
+ 61 pp; 11 Alan & Sandy Carey/OSF; 12 Anup
Shah/naturepl.com; 15 Lynn M. Stone/naturepl.com;
19 Erwin & Peggy Bauer/BCC; 21 T. Andrewartha/
Frank Lane Picture Agency; 24–25 John Downer/
OSF; 31 Rafi Ben-Shahar/OSF; 39 R. & M. van
Nostrand/Frank Lane Picture Agency; 45 Carlos
Sanchez/OSF; 47 Dr. R.E. Stebbings; 68–69 John
Hartley/NHPA; 72–73 Aldo Brando/OSF; 77 Andrea
Florence/Ardea London; 93 Clive Bromhall/OSF; 95
Daniel J. Cox/OSF; 97 Konrad Wothe/OSF; 98–99
Dave Watts; 104–105 Jean-Paul Ferrero/Ardea
London; 111 A.N.T./NHPA; 127 Stephen Mills/OSF;
165 & 169 Daniel Heuclin/NHPA; 173 Animals
Animals/Dr. Mark A. Chappell/OSF; 177 Mark
Jones/OSF; 179 Mark Webster/OSF; 181 Nick
Gordon/OSF; 183 Animals Animals/Zig Leszczynski/
OSF; 187 Michael Fogden/OSF; 191 Robert &
Valerie Davies; 193 Animals Animals/Zig
Leszczynski/OSF; 195 Mike Linley/OSF; 197 Robin
Bush/OSF; 199 Ken Preston-Mafham/Premaphotos
Wildlife; 201 Jane Burton/BCC; 203 Orion Press/
BCC; 205 P. Morris/Ardea London; 215 Fredrik
Ehrenstrom/OSF; 217 Animals Animals/Carl
Roessler/OSF; 219 Tony Bomford/OSF; 221 Peter
Scoones/Science Photo Library; 241 Fredrik
Ehrenstrom/OSF; 243 David B. Fleetham/OSF; 247
Rod Williams/BCC; Animals Animals/Breck P.
Kent/OSF.

POCKET FACTFILES
Endangered Animals

Sterling Publishing Co., Inc.
New York

CONTENTS

REPTILES 174

AMPHIBIANS 194

FISH 206

INSECTS AND INVERTEBRATES 234

GLOSSARY 250 INDEX 254

WHAT IS AN ENDANGERED SPECIES?

Any animal whose numbers are in sharp decline and under so much threat that it may totally disappear from this planet is an endangered species. Tigers and panda bears are high profile examples that often spring to mind, but there are thousands of lesser-known animals – equally if not more under threat from hunting, habitat loss, pollution, climate change, changes in the food chain, disease, and many other factors.

  We know they are under threat because wildlife and conservation organizations study their populations, breeding, behavior, and lifestyles and can use special computer software to predict if numbers are going down. Pressure groups such as Greenpeace and Friends of the Earth draw attention to the plight of wildlife by staging stunts that attract the media, governments,

LEVELS OF THREAT
Under the IUCN, each species is given a level of threat based on its closeness to extinction. This is also given for each entry in this book:

EX=Extinct
As dead as the dodo – when there is no hope of a species still surviving

EW=Extinct in the Wild
Only surviving in captivity (e.g. a zoo or by re-introduction somewhere outside its former location)

CR=Critically Endangered
At high risk of extinction with less than 50 to 250 individuals depending on a stable or declining population. Also animals with a larger population which have declined by 80 percent.

EN= Endangered
Species with few numbers, from 250 to 2,500 depending if the population is stable or declining; also where the range is under 1,900 sq m (5,000 sq km) and the population levels are declining.

VU=Vulnerable
A high risk, but not on an immediate level. Less than 1,000 individuals in a stable population or 10,000 if the population is declining. Other measures include a range of less than 772 sq m (20,000 sq km) or 10 per cent chance of extinction in 10 years.

LR= Lower Risk
Evaluated but not judged to be life threatened.

and corporations into some form of action and response. Sadly, the decline has become so dramatic for so many species that an international conservation body now coordinates research and information on threatened animals around the world and provides support to local initiatives in individual countries.

The IUCN

Also known as the World Conservation Union, the International Union for the Conservation of Nature (IUCN) has over 1,000 permanent staff and over 10,000 volunteers from 181 countries supporting initiatives on protected areas, eco-system management, education, environmental law, and projects to help species survive. Its Species Survival Commission (SSC) has thousands of experts studying plant and animal conservation. It produces an invaluable reference of species under threat with its regularly updated "red lists" (first published in 1966) and now in CD-ROM format and on the Internet.

CONSERVING WILDLIFE
Many threatened species could be lost forever in just our lifetime. International organizations both monitor their status *(right, IUCN red list)*, which is vital, and work "on the ground" *(left, with kiwis)* to protect endangered animals.

Measuring the Danger

Some 18,000 species are on the pages, of which over 11,000 are threatened with extinction. The red lists cannot force a government to protect any endangered animals, but they do help governments make informed decisions when assessing conservation priorities. The red lists form the basis for the categories of threat used in this book.

CITES

The other key measure of a species' population status is provided by the Convention on International Trade in Endangered Species of Wild Fauna and Flora (otherwise known as CITES). It is also called the Washington Convention – after the U.S. capital where the convention was originally signed in 1975 by some 150 nations. The convention prohibits the hunting and trading of animals and body parts – a big factor in the decline of some rare species. A convention acts as an international law – in this case by having three agreed appendices which are reviewed every few years and which the countries that signed must follow. (Of course countries that haven't signed, such as Iraq, Albania and North Korea can continue to trade and hunt to extinction.)

DEGREES OF THREAT
Threatened mammals species = 1,130 (out of c. 4,750, or 24 percent);
4 percent are Critically Endangered; one-quarter are significantly threatened.
Since the 1700s, around 90 mammals species have become extinct.
Threatened birds species = 1,186 (out of c. 9,760). Critically Endangered 182
Threatened fish species = 752 (out of over 20,000). Critically Endangered 156
Threatened insect species = 555 (out of 950,000 species)

MAJOR THREATS TO WILDLIFE ON THIS PLANET

Habitat loss

With 6 billion humans on the planet – and rising – we are the biggest threat to animals as we take over wild and natural habitats for farming, industry, housing, and larger and larger cities. Tourism, and the development that goes with it, often in coastal, mountainous, and remote world locations is a growing problem.

Hunting

Whales and elephants are just two obvious examples of animals brought to the verge of extinction by hunters after their body parts. But today even the humble cod has been devastated by over-fishing. The trade in rare birds, eggs, and feathers is worrying.

Civil wars and refugees

Human upheavals cause the death of many animals and of course make conservation projects dangerous.

Trade in live animals

In 1996 alone, the U.S. imported over 1.7 million reptiles (including over 694,000 iguanas). The aquarium trade has also wiped out millions of fish and amphibians. Animals separated from their mother and natural habitat will have a slimmer chance of survival.

Pollution and climate change

An oil tanker spillage can kill 1,000 sea otters, 300,000 seabirds and millions of fish in one fell swoop. Acid rain and pesticides do even more harm over a longer time.

LEOPARD

Panthera pardus
Family: FELIDAE
Order: CARNIVORA

STATUS: Varies with subspecies: lower risk to critical. Isolated North African leopard (*Panthera pardus panthera*), for example, is Critical. All leopards CITES I. World population probably far fewer than the 700,000 estimated in 1988.

DISTRIBUTION: Diverse habitat, from forests to open spaces, anywhere where there is sufficient food and cover. Largest populations in sub-Saharan Africa, with scattered and shrinking populations in northern Africa and parts of Asia.

SIZE: Length, head and body, 35–75in (90–190cm); tail 22–42in (58–110cm); height to shoulder 17.5–31in (45–78cm); males up to 50% bigger than females. Weight 61–200lb (28–90kg).

FORM: Large pale-buff to deep chestnut cat, marked with dark rosettes on body and tail; head marked with smaller spots, belly and legs with large blotches. Black ones are known as black panthers.

DIET: Mostly hoofed animals such as gazelles, wildebeest, goats, and pigs; also takes monkeys, rodents, rabbits, birds, and invertebrates.

BREEDING: Between 1 and 6 (usually 2 or 3) cubs born after gestation of 13–15 weeks at any time of year in Africa, more seasonal elsewhere. Weaned at 3 months; mature at 3 years. May live over 20 years.

CONSERVATION: Provided there is a plentiful supply of food and secure cover to rest, rear its young and hide during the day, the leopard remains adaptable and widespread in different climates and habitats. In sub-Saharan Africa it is still relatively numerous, especially in national parks like Serengeti. Elsewhere poaching for fur, persecution by farmers, and loss of habitat have brought several subspecies to the brink of extinction. The leopard is legally protected in almost every country in its range, although several nations still allow limited hunting – totalling up to 2,000 kills a year. This is probably sustainable, compared to the 50,000-a-year killed in the 1960s and 1970s.

BIG CAT ON THE EDGE
Five leopard subspecies, from northwestern Africa across to the Middle East, Siberia, and Korea are listed as Critically Endangered – with some populations less than 250. Four other subspecies are listed as Endangered.

TIGER

Panthera tigris
Family: FELIDAE
Order: CARNIVORA

STATUS: Endangered (IUCN); CITIES I. Around 5,000 7,000 tigers survive.

DISTRIBUTION: Dense cover, tall grass thickets and mangroves from India east to China and Vietnam and south to Indonesia (Sumatra).

SIZE: length head/body: 4.5–9ft (1.4–2.7m); tail: 24–43in (60–110cm); height at shoulder: 31–43in (80–110cm). Weight: up to 790lb (360kg) in the largest Siberian tigers.

FORM: Striking, large orange cat with black stripes and long tail.

DIET: Mostly deer and wild pigs weighing 110–440lb (50–200kg). Occasionally monkeys, fish, and even small birds. Needs about 33–40lb (15–18kg) per day.

BREEDING: Two or 3 cubs per litter, born after 14-week gestation. Life span 15 years in the wild, at least 26 in captivity.

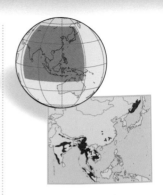

SHARP DECLINE
The tiger used to occur across Asia as far west as Turkey, but in the last 100 years numbers have declined sharply. There are about 4,500 tigers remaining in India, the species' main stronghold.

CONSERVATION: Tigers need to kill to eat and will kill domestic animals and even people. This has led to the tigers themselves being hunted. Their own habitat has been reduced by farming and logging to the point where natural prey is difficult to find in sufficient quantity. Humans hunt the same prey, leaving little food for the tigers. Nevertheless, tigers are unlikely to become extinct as they breed well in captivity. However, the captive population has become seriously inbred in the past, and there has been genetic mixing between the five subspecies. In addition, tigers cost a lot to feed, so most zoos control the numbers of young born. The future lies in management of the remaining tiger habitats and reserves. Conservation measures will include linking small, isolated groups of animals and preventing poaching and further habitat loss. It is also vital to have plenty of prey animals. Huge areas of land need to be set aside to maintain the numbers of prey needed to support just a few tigers. The dangers of inbreeding may be reduced by using captive-bred animals as a fresh gene source.

FLORIDA PANTHER

Puma concolor coryi
Family: FELIDAE
Order: CARNIVORA

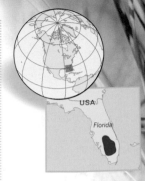

USA

Florida

STATUS: Critical (IUCN), CITES I. Between 30 and 50 survive Related endangered species: Eastern panther (*Puma concolor cougar*)

DISTRIBUTION: Swampland with dense bush and palmetto (small palm) thickets in and around the Everglades National Park and Cypress National Preserve of South central Florida.

SIZE: Length head/body 42–54in (100–130cm); tail 30–36in (72–80cm); height at shoulder 26–31in (62–75cm). Weight 66–125lb (30–57kg).

FORM: Large, tawny or dark-brown cat with white flecks around the shoulders; long black-tipped tail, sharply kinked toward the end. Black on sides of face and backs of ears.

DIET: Deer; also hares, rodents, armadillos; occasionally domestic and farm animals.

BREEDING: One to 6 (usually 3) cubs born at almost any time of year. Gestation period of about 3 months; mature at 2–3 years.

CONSERVATION: Take away the pressures of farmers creating new farmland, the highways slicing through the remaining habitat, and the scale of domestic and industrial pollutants in Florida and there might have been a healthy population of over 1,000 panthers. As it is, the handful of handsome panthers left cling perilously to their remaining habitat despite being legally protected since 1973. Ultimately the panther needs a wide area – 18 to 50 miles (30–80km) – to hunt and live in. This is simply not viable with fenced-off highways, fast-moving traffic and farmland eating into the

swamplands. Crop irrigation and new town water supplies have dried up vast areas of swamp making them more at risk to forest fires. This in turn removes vital cover and drives away the panthers' prey such as deer. Import of females from the Texan Panther subspecies and a special sperm bank are two measures set up to encourage breeding.

BREEDING PROBLEMS
A major problem for the remaining 50 or so Florida panthers is their interbeeding with more common cougars, which threatens their status as a protected subspecies.

THYLACINE

Thylacinus cynocephalus
Family: THYLACINIDAE
Order: DASYUROMORPHIA

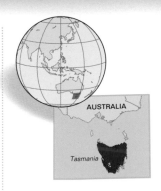

AUSTRALIA

Tasmania

STATUS: Extinct (IUCN), CITES I. No close relatives.

DISTRIBUTION: Once inhabited open woodland in mainland Australia and Tasmania.

SIZE: Length, head and body, 35–50in (90–130cm); tail 20–25in (50–65cm); height to shoulder 14–24in (35–60cm); males larger than females. Weight up to about 40lb (18kg).

FORM: Resembled a large, heavy, sandy-colored dog, with bold black stripes across its haunches. Long, stiff tail. Also known as the Tasmanian Wolf or Tasmanian Tiger.

DIET: Small wallabies and kangaroos; probably also smaller mammals, birds and reptiles.

BREEDING: 2–3 young born from December to March. A marsupial, it had a rear-facing pouch housing 4 nipples. Life span in wild unknown; 13 years in captivity.

CONSERVATION: Once common across Australia and Tasmania, this large marsupial was a surprisingly slow-moving and clumsy creature. The thylacine also lacked a strong bite and when

domestic dogs and other introduced animals reached Australia, it
was unable to compete with these
more efficient hunters. It soon died
out. The thylacine's rapid decline
was spurred on by European
settlers from the 1840s onwards.
They not only changed the habitat
by introducing sheep farming, but
also persecuted the thylacine since
they considered it to be a serious
pest. By 1910 it was confined to
Tasmania and even with legal
protection from 1936, it was
probably already extinct in the wild.
There are still occasional reported
sightings, but there has been no
concrete evidence that the thylacine
is still alive. In Tasmania a large
area of the animal's former habitat
– hilly terrain in dense forest – has
been set aside as a protected
reserve in case any have survived.
Recreating a thylacine by cloning
remains a remote possibility.

LAST OF THE THYLACINES
The last wild thylacine
was captured in 1933
and lived alone in a zoo
in Tasmania, where it
died in 1936. Since then
no thylacine has been
found, dead or alive,
but reported sightings
are still investigated
seriously.

SWIFT FOX

Vulpes velox
Family: CANIDAE
Order: CARNIVORA

STATUS: Lower risk, conservation dependent (IUCN), not listed by CITES. Related endangered species include red wolf (*Canis rufus*) and African wild dog (*Lycaon pictus*).

DISTRIBUTION: Confined to open plains and deserts of western U.S.; was extinct in Canada but has been reintroduced.

SIZE: Length, head and body, 15–20in (36–48cm); tail 9–12in (22–30cm). Weight 4–6lb (1.8–2.7kg).

FORM: Small, large-eared, buff-yellow fox with black markings on either side of muzzle and bushy tail with black tip.

DIET: Small mammals, mainly rodents, occasionally large insects.

BREEDING: Between 4 and 7 pups born between February and April. Life span up to 7 years in the wild, 20 years in captivity.

CONSERVATION: Swift foxes used to be found in open prairie and desert habitats from Canada in the north to the Mexican border in the south. Their numbers dwindled in the northerly states when much of their habitat was taken over as farmland. The swift fox population also suffered heavy losses as a result of trapping and poisoning campaigns intended to eradicate other more abundant carnivores that were thought to be a threat to livestock – ironically, the swift fox is a nocturnal hunter that feeds on rabbits, rats, and mice and as such is a help to farmers.

The animal is also relatively tame and was easy to trap for its fur, while others were killed on the roads or fell prey to the coyote – a larger relative and the main predator of swift fox cubs. As a result it eventually became extinct in Canada. Attempts to reintroduce the swift fox into the country began in the early 1980s. From 1983 to 1997 hundreds of

PURSUED BY POISON
A member of the dog family, the small swift fox was nearly wiped out when it became the unwitting victim of poisoning campaigns. Far from being a pest, the swift fox feeds on rodents and does not harm chickens or other livestock. Numbers today are in the low thousands.

foxes were raised in captivity and taken to Canada, together with 91 captured wild foxes, for release into 17 selected sites. However, by 1997 the total Canadian population was still fewer than 200. The project has been criticized, since none of the animals released were of Canadian stock, all coming from the south. In addition, research shows that swift foxes are slowly spreading northward on their own, suggesting that recolonization of suitable areas will eventually take place naturally, without the need for human intervention.

POLAR BEAR

Ursus maritimus
Family: URSIDAE
Order: CARNIVORA

North Pole

STATUS: Lower risk, conservation dependent (IUCN), CITES II. World population 20,000–30,000. Related endangered species: spectacled bear (*Tremarctos ornatus*), and sloth bear (*Melursus ursinus*).

DISTRIBUTION: Arctic ice floes in the Polar regions of Russia, Norway (Svalbard and Jan Mayen), Greenland, Canada, and the U.S. (Alaska).

SIZE: Length 8.2–11.5ft (2.5–3.5m); height at shoulder when on all fours 42in (107cm); males larger than females. Weight: females 660lb (300kg), males 1,100–1,320lb (500–600kg).

FORM: A huge, stocky bear with proportionately small head, furry ears, short tail, and big, furry feet. The fur is thick and creamy-white to dirty yellow.

BREEDING: Between 1 and 4 cubs (usually 2) born from December to January.

DIET: Mainly ringed and bearded seals and the occasional young walrus; will also eat carrion, eggs, rodents, berries, and just about anything it can find.

CONSERVATION: Perhaps the most striking feature of the polar bear is its thick, white coat – the perfect color for an Arctic predator in the snowy wastes. The bear's black nose can give it away however, and there are stories of polar bears stalking seals while trying to cover their noses. Polar bears are the largest land carnivores (meat-eaters). They have excellent eyesight, a superb sense of smell to detect young seals hidden in the ice, and are massively strong, efficient hunters. True nomads, they often hitch a ride on a drifting ice floe, traveling many miles at a time, often across international borders. These solitary creatures were always scarce, and they suffered from severe, uncontrolled hunting during the 20th century.

Until the 1960s, when the five polar bear nations (Russia, Canada, Greenland, Norway, and the U.S.) signed a conservation treaty, it was difficult to protect them or to research populations. Numbers have increased since then and today's population seems stable, with most of the bears living in northern Canada. Controlled hunting is regulated: if it were not, the bear would become endangered because of its slow rate of population growth. Apart from hunters, who cull around 700 bears a year worldwide, the main threats to the species are increasing pollution and the prospect of climate warming.

LARGEST LAND CARNIVORE
The polar bear may cover a range of over 100,000 sq. miles (260,000 sq. km) in its lifetime. It inhabits the ice-edge, walking the floes or swimming the channels. It can leap over 6ft (2m) from water to ice floe.

GIANT PANDA

Ailuropoda melanoleuca
Family: URSIDAE
Order: CARNIVORA

STATUS: Endangered (IUCN), CITES II. World population down to about 1,000.

DISTRIBUTION: The cool, mountain bamboo forests found in the central provinces of China.

SIZE: Length, head and body, 4–5ft (1.2–1.5m); tail about 5in (12–13cm); height at shoulder about 24in (60cm). Weight 165–350lb (75–160kg).

FORM: A stocky, bearlike animal with creamy-white fur on its body but with black fur on its legs, shoulders, ears, and around eyes.

DIET: Mainly bamboo, but also other plant materials. Occasionally, fish and small animals.

BREEDING: They breed very slowly, as females are fertile for only 2–3 days in a year. Up to 3 young are born at a time, but normally only 1 survives. Pandas take at least 5 years to reach

maturity and may not breed every year. They live for up to 34 years in captivity, much less in the wild.

CONSERVATION: The giant panda is one of the most instantly recognizable animals in the world;

yet probably fewer than 100 have ever been seen alive outside China. In the past, giant pandas were hunted because their body parts were believed to have magical properties. Today, the giant panda is under threat because its bamboo forest habitat, on the lower mountain slopes, has been carved up to make way for farmland and human settlement. Logging is also damaging the animal's forest feeding ground. The giant panda needs to consume a huge quantity of bamboo – it can chew through 600 bamboo stems in a day. Therefore the contraction of its bamboo habitat causes the bear serious problems. The situation is made worse by the bamboo's habit of flowering every so often and then dying – a phenomenon that appears to be on the increase. In the 1970s, when three species of bamboo died at once, over 100 pandas (more than a tenth of the population) starved to death. Nowadays the population is fairly stable, though perilously small and fragmented. Special sanctuaries have been created and the animal is protected under Chinese law.

HIGH-PROFILE SPECIES
The giant panda has come to symbolize all endangered animals and Man's efforts to save them. Fittingly, it is the emblem of the World Wide Fund for Nature (WWF) – a highly familiar emblem worldwide.

BLACK RHINOCEROS

Diceros bicornis
Family: RHINOCEROTIDAE
Order: PERISSODACTYLA

STATUS: Critical (IUCN). World population estimated at about 2,000. Related endangered species include white rhinoceros (*Ceratotherium simum*) and great Indian rhinoceros (*Rhinoceros unicornis*).

DISTRIBUTION: Savanna and bush in Africa south of the Sahara, in widely scattered localities. Rarely found more than a day's walk from a water supply.

SIZE: Length, head and body, 9.5–12.3ft (2.9–3.7m); tail 24–28in (60–70cm); height at shoulder 4.5–5.9ft (1.4–1.8m). Weight 1,500–3,000lb (700–1,400kg).

FORM: Large, thick-skinned animal, grayish in color but often coated with mud. Two horns on the snout and a pointed, mobile upper lip, used to gather food.

DIET: Leaves, twigs, and branches browsed from more than 200 species of low-growing shrub.

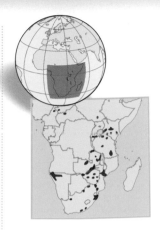

BACK FROM THE BRINK
Hunted for dagger handles and oriental medicine, virtually to extinction, the black rhinoceros now numbers some 2,000. These slow-breeding animals survive mainly in fenced sanctuaries in East and Southern Africa.

BREEDING: A very slow reproduction rate, one baby every 3–5 years, makes this rhino ill-equipped to cope with population loss. Single calf born after 15-month gestation; suckled for up to 1 year. Life span to 40 years.

CONSERVATION: Once widespread in Africa, black rhinoceros numbers have been reduced by 97 percent since the 1970s. Man is the culprit, specifically with the international trade in rhino horn. For centuries rhino horn, composed of densely compressed hair, has been used in oriental medicine as a remedy for various disorders. In fact the horn material is made of keratin which cannot be absorbed into the body. Despite this, the horns continue to fetch high prices. There has also been an increase in demand from oil-rich Yemen. Here the horns are used for making carved dagger handles which are regarded as a status symbol. Although the rhinos are under legal protection, the lucrative and lethal trade in horns has continued, and the species has died out in many areas. Efforts have been made to encourage alternative sources for horn, such as cow and buffalo, and another conservation strategy is to humanely cut off the horns and thereby remove the poachers' incentive.

JAVAN RHINOCEROS

Rhinoceros sondaicus
Family: RHINOCEROTIDAE
Order: PERISSODACTYLA

STATUS: Critical (IUCN), CITES I. World population probably fewer than 80. Related endangered species include the Sumatran rhinoceros (*Dicerorhinus sumatrensis*) and black rhinoceros (*Diceros bicornis*).

DISTRIBUTION: Dense thickets of reed, bamboo, and tall grasses in the damp tropical forests of Java in Indonesia, Vietnam, and perhaps Cambodia, or Laos.

SIZE: Length, head and body, 10–10.5ft (3–3.2m); tail 28in (70cm); height at shoulder 5–5.8ft (1.6–1.8m); female larger than male. Weight 3,200–4,400lb (1,500–2,000kg).

FORM: A huge animal with knobby skin that hangs in large, stiff sections like sheets of armor plate. There is a single horn, usually less than 6in (15cm) long.

DIET: Leaves, bark, and twigs stripped from trees; fallen fruit.

BREEDING: A single calf is born at 4–5 year intervals, after gestation of 16 months. It suckles for up to 2 years and takes 4–6 years to reach maturity. A life span of over 20 years is possible.

CONSERVATION: The Javan rhinoceros is at risk of extinction mainly because its favored, steamy forest habitat has been cleared, drained, and developed by farmers to raise cattle and grow crops. Another threat to the rhino is the continual demand for rhino horn in Eastern medicine, famously for use as an aphrodisiac. Like other rhinos, the Javan species has been hunted for centuries, even though males have one small horn and females often lack them. The Vietnam War also reduced numbers drastically and a group of about 60 rhinos in an Indonesian national park may now be the only fairly safe population. There is hope that as Laos and Cambodia recover after decades of war, more rhinos may be found. The danger is that economic recovery may encourage rural development, which in turn will reduce numbers once more.

TANK UNDER THREAT
The single-horned Javan rhino may seem built like a tank but it is still under threat: there are none in captivity that can be returned to the wild if needed.

MALAYAN TAPIR

Tapirus indicus
Family: TAPIRIDAE
Order: PERISSODACTYLA

STATUS: Vulnerable (IUCN), CITES I. World population unknown, perhaps up to 5,000. Related endangered species: Central American tapir *(Tapirus bairdii)* and mountain tapir *(T. pinchaque)*.

DISTRIBUTION: Dense tropical rain forest and grasslands by water in Myanmar (Burma), Thailand, mainland Malaysia, and Sumatra.

SIZE: Length 6–9ft (1.8–2.7m); height at shoulder 29–47in (73–120cm). Weight 330–700lb (150–320kg).

FORM: Robust, piglike animal with long, fleshy snout and short, sturdy legs. Striking markings: white body, with black head and legs.

DIET: Grass, leaves of shrubs and aquatic plants; also seeks salt licks.

BREEDING: Single young born every other year in May–June after 13–14 month gestation; mature at 3 years. May live up to 30 years.

CONSERVATION: The black-and-white tapirs of Southeast Asia are thinly distributed among small "islands" of habitat. As the tapir's pristine jungle home is cleared away to make way for farmland and human settlement, the tapir is placed in an increasingly vulnerable position. Man is also the tapir's most dangerous predator – tapirs are prized for their flesh, and their meat is often sold illegally for a high price. There is also a continued trade in live animals. Tapirs seem to take to captivity well, making them popular with private collectors. One consolation is that as tapirs breed well in captivity, they are unlikely to become extinct. On the other hand, the continued illegal trade threatens the vulnerable wild population. To date the tapir has been far less researched than many other New World species. However, the tapir shares part of its range with several high-profile endangered predators which poses something of a conservation puzzle. Meanwhile, their decline removes one of the key species involved in dispersing the seeds of large trees.

STRIKING MARKINGS
The Malayan tapir's black and white markings help the animal blend in well with the bright pools of moonlight and deep shadows at night.

PYGMY HIPPOPOTAMUS

Hexaprotodon liberiensis
Family: HIPPOPOTAMIDAE
Order: ARTIODACTYLA

STATUS: Vulnerable (IUCN), CITES II. World population numbers a few thousand. Related endangered species: common hippopotamus subspecies (*Hippopotamus amphibius tschadensis*) of Chad and Niger.

DISTRIBUTION: Swamps and lowland forests of Liberia, Sierra Leone, Nigeria, Ivory Coast, and Guinea.

SIZE: Length 5–5.6ft (1.5–1.7m); height at shoulder 30–40in (75–100cm). Weight 355–600lb (160–270kg).

FORM: Similar to common hippopotamus but about one tenth the size. Skin hairless and shiny, greenish brown to dark slate gray.

DIET: Leaves, shoots, roots, and fruit.

BREEDING: Single young (very occasionally twins) born at any time of year after 7-month gestation; weaned at 6–8 months; mature at 4–5 years. Life span up to 35 years.

CONSERVATION: Hunting and habitat destruction are the key threats to the pygmy hippo line. The meat of pygmy hippos is much sought after and since the animal is much less aggressive than the larger and more dangerous common hippo, it is easy prey. Pygmy hippos live alone to avoid the attention of predators. This strategy however requires plenty of hiding space and, as logging takes its toll on the forest, the number of areas capable of supporting hippo life has seriously declined. The population is now found only in a few scattered areas of West Africa.

and is rare wherever it occurs. Political turmoil, in places such as Sierra Leone, has also put the future of the pygmy hippo in severe doubt. The one glimmer of hope is that well over 300 hippos have taken easily to life in captivity, offering the hope that they can be reintroduced to the wild when environmental and political conditions in their natural range improve.

HARMLESS HIPPO
The glossy pygmy hippopotamus lives alone to keep out of trouble – but it cannot avoid the ravages of war that have disturbed much of its swampy habitat.

SIBERIAN MUSK DEER

Moschus moschiferus
Family: MOSCHIDAE
Order: ARTIODACTYLA

STATUS: Vulnerable (IUCN), CITES I and II, according to country location. World population about 100,000, but spread over a huge area. Related endangered species include forest musk deer (*Moschus berezovskii*), and black musk deer (*M. fuscus*)

DISTRIBUTION: Mountain forests up to 5,000ft (1,600m) above sea level in Siberia, Manchuria, Korea, China, and Sakhalin Island; some in Mongolia.

SIZE: Length 30–36in (76.2–91cm); height 20–21in (50–55cm); males often smaller than females. Weight 24–30lb (11–14kg).

FORM: Hind legs longer than forelegs, so the rump is higher than the shoulders, and the back appears arched. The coat is spotted when young, but adults are a dark grayish brown. They have no antlers. Males have sharp canine teeth that point downward like small tusks.

DIET: Mostly lichens, but also leaves, conifer needles, and tree bark. A range of herbaceous plants in summer; also some grasses.

BREEDING: Breeding season November–December; 1 or (rarely) 2 young born in June of the following year. Can live up to 20 years in captivity.

CONSERVATION: Siberian musk deer are small, solitary, mountain-dwelling deer that have been ruthlessly hunted for their musk – a scent produced only by the males, probably to attract females. Musk was a highly valued ingredient first for medicinal use, then later for perfumes and soaps. Although international trade in musk glands is prohibited – and a synthetic substitute is available – musk still fetches high prices on the black market and over 5,000 male musk deers may be killed every year. The females do not produce musk. However, poachers

make no distinction and kill them too. In one year 100,000 musk glands were imported into Japan alone. As a result, the total population is thought to have halved during the 1990s. To make matters worse, forests have been cleared for timber and farming. Luckily, there is still enough habitat, but numbers are falling. The only real solution is to stop the trade in musk totally.

FASHION VICTIM
One male musk deer holds a mere 1 ounce (28g) of musk – used as a base for perfumes. The musk could be extracted from a living animal, but poachers shoot the deer rather than capture them alive. Until the trade is halted, every musk deer is vulnerable.

JENTINK'S DUIKER

Cephalophus jentinki
Family: BOVIDAE
Order: ARTIODACTYLA

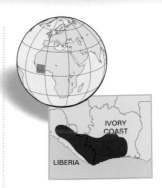

STATUS: Vulnerable (IUCN), CITES 1. World population fewer than 2,000. Related endangered species: Ruwenzori black-fronted duiker (*Cephalophus nigrifrons*), and Ader's duiker (*C. adersi*).

DISTRIBUTION: Dense forests and scrub in Sierra Leone, Liberia, and Ivory Coast.

SIZE: Length 4.5ft (1.4m); height at shoulder 30–33in (75–80cm). Weight up to 155lb (70kg).

FORM: Slight, short-horned antelope with short legs and slightly arched back. Coat distinctively patterned: dark head and neck, white collar, grizzled gray back, and pale legs; narrow crest of tufty fur on head.

DIET: Mostly plant material, including leaves, shoots, and fruit; some insects, carrion, birds' eggs.

BREEDING: Single young born after 7.5 months. The baby is weaned at 5 months; female matures at 9–12 months, male at 12–18 months. Life span up to 12 years.

CONSERVATION: Jentink's duiker is not only rare, it is also extremely shy. It only comes out at night. The name "duiker" comes from the Afrikaans word meaning "diver," describing how it darts for cover at the slightest disturbance. Sadly, the increased sightings are only a sign that humans are encroaching on the duiker's territory, forcing the animals from the forest and out into the open. In fact, the greatest threat to Jentink's duiker is hunting for bush meat. Being the largest of the duikers, Jentink's is more at risk from hunting than its smaller relatives.

Despite legal protection from commercial hunting, it is impossible to stop local people from hunting for the meat. The problem is more serious where large numbers of people come to work in the forests. In Sierra Leone, civil war has seen soldiers as well as loggers killing duikers to live off the land. Better public education and protection of the animals and their habitats offer Jentink's duiker the only chances of survival in a poor and politically volatile part of the world.

DARTING AND DIVING
Jentink's duiker hides in forest and thickets during the day, protecting its offspring from the local hunters who are after their meat. The duiker comes out to feed at night, when its patterned coat makes it difficult to see in the moonlight.

KOUPREY

Bos sauveli
Family: BOVIDAE
Order: ARTIODACTYLA

STATUS: Critical (IUCN), CITES I. Fewer than 300 in the world. Related endangered species include lowland anoa (*Bubalus depressicornis*), and wild yak (*Bos grunniens*).

DISTRIBUTION: Forest edges and thickets in rolling hill country, retreating to denser forests, in Cambodia and Vietnam. Once found in Malaysia and Thailand.

SIZE: Length 7–7.2ft (2.1–2.2m); height at shoulder 5.5–6.2ft (1.7–1.9m). Weight up to 1,500–2,000lb (700–910kg).

FORM: A large, gray ox with distinctive horns: lyre-shaped in females, curved with frayed edges in males.

DIET: Mostly grasses, but also some leaves.

BREEDING: Single calf born between December and February. May live for about 20 years.

CONSERVATION. The kouprey is one of the world's rarest mammals. Its chances of survival were put back a step when the region it inhabited suffered prolonged military action. By the mid-1970s numbers had plummeted, but the species somehow managed to struggle through. These days most of the population is thought to live in Cambodia, often mingling with other wild cattle such as water buffalo, or even domestic herds. It is possible koupreys may be resistant to the cattle disease, rinderpest, which should add to the impetus to save the species (as their immunity might provide a basis for a vaccine). Despite international cooperation, the sheer scarcity of these shy oxen is hindering efforts to monitor and protect them. Meanwhile logging and forest clearing continue to erode their habitat.

BIG-HORNED FOREST OX
The kouprey has not been lucky in its distribution. Warfare in Cambodia, where it is mostly found, has hampered efforts to preserve it. The best solution would appear to be properly protected reserves and the building of a captive-breeding program.

SCIMITAR-HORNED ORYX

Oryx dammah
Family: BOVIDAE
Order: ARTIODACTYLA

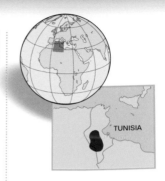

TUNISIA

STATUS: Extinct in the wild (IUCN), CITES I. World population unknown, possibly fewer than 500 with over 1,000 in zoos worldwide.

DISTRIBUTION: Formerly widespread, now reintroduced population in southern Tunisia. Large numbers semiwild on game ranches in Texas; some also in Israel. Habitat hot, dry semidesert, with grassy patches among dunes and scattered acacia trees.

SIZE: Length, head and body, 6.6–7.6ft (1.9–2.2m); tail 18–24in (45–60cm); height at shoulder 47–52in (110–120cm). Weight about 300lb (135kg), but up to 480lb (216kg) in captivity.

FORM: Pale fawn and white, deepchested antelope with elegant, long, sharp, backward-curving horns that have rings around them. Face long; tail long and hairy.

DIET: Mostly grass, but also other vegetation, fruit, and seed pods.

BREEDING: Single calf, gestation period 7.5–8 months. Life span in captivity over 17 years.

CONSERVATION: The scimitar-horned oryx is on the verge of extinction in its native Africa. The northern population became extinct over a century ago. The main threat to the southern population is not local trophy hunters, but the expansion of the Sahara Desert. This has caused the loss of grazing grass. Other grazing domestic animals also compete with this oryx, and the removal of trees for fuel has speeded up soil erosion. In north Africa, the Tunisian government is committed to reviving the oryx population by protecting its habitat, imposing limits on domestic livestock, and reintroducing oryx from zoo stock.

DOUBLE THREAT
The Oryx faces
extinction from
encroaching desert
and domestic animals
which compete for
what is left of
grazing land.

Vu Quang Ox

Pseudoryx nghetinhensis
Family: BOVIDAE
Order: ARTIODACTYLA

STATUS: Endangered (IUCN), CITES I. World population unknown, probably only a few hundred at most. Related endangered species: Saiga (*Saiga tatarica*) a type of Asian goat.

DISTRIBUTION: Dense mountain forests up to 6,500ft (2,000m) stretching 1,500sq m (4,000sq km), between Laos and Vietnam.

SIZE: Length, head and body, 5–6.7ft (1.5–2m); tail 5in (13cm); height at shoulder 2.7–3ft (80–90cm). Weight 200 lb (90kg).

FORM: Dark-brown antelopelike animal with white "socks", white eyebrows, and spots on the face, chin, and nose. Brown tail with cream band and black tip. Prominent scent gland forms a slit in front of each eye. Thin horns that curve slightly backward and are up to 20 in (50cm) long.

DIET: Leaves browsed from low shrubs; also grass.

BREEDING: Probably only 1 young born per year in February or March.

CONSERVATION: In spite of its considerable size, the Vu Quang ox only came to light in 1992. One reason for its obscurity – and survival – was its remote forest home in the steep mountain slopes of the Vu Quang Reserve between Laos and Vietnam. Parts are government protected but local hunters still kill the oxen for meat.

While endless wars in the region once discouraged settlers, peace has returned, and with it pressure to develop the slopes, thereby posing new problems for this extremely endangered species.

REMOTE HIDEAWAY
The small, pony-sized Vu Quang ox has been protected from the rest of the world by its remote Asian mountain habitat – but today even the most secluded parts of its range are at risk from human exploitation.

GRAY BAT

Myotis grisescens
Family: VESPERTILIONIDAE
Order: CHIROPTERA

STATUS: Endangered (IUCN), not listed by CITES. World population about 1.6–2 million, but concentrated in a few places. More than 20 other species of *Myotis* are under serious threat.

DISTRIBUTION: Roosts in caves in southern and eastern U.S., especially Alabama and Tennessee. Feeds over water and open habitats.

SIZE: Length, head and body, 3-3.7in (8–9.5cm); tail about 1in (2.5cm); wingspan about 14in (35cm). Weight 0.3–0.6oz (7–16g).

FORM: Largest *Myotis* bat in eastern U.S. Fur gray with all the hairs on the back uniform in color (other bats have brown or pale tips to the hairs); wing membrane joins foot at the ankle.

DIET: Insects, especially aquatic ones, such as mayflies.

BREEDING: Single young born per year. Life span up to 20 years.

CONSERVATION: The gray bat hibernates and roosts in just a few caves, where it is extremely vulnerable to disturbance and destruction. The biggest and best caves are limestone but unfortunately this stone is valuable so it is extensively quarried, destroying caves in the process.

Tourists visiting caves also pose a threat as their noise can disturb hibernating bats. A bat disturbed during hibernation raises its body temperature to normal levels by using up fat reserves. If a bat is woken up too many times during the winter, it will not have enough fat to last until spring. Vandals, too, cause problems – they attack clusters of bats. The bats are defenseless, unable to fly until their bodies warm up, and young bats

FURRY GRAY BATS
Innocently huddled in
caves, these rare bats
seem to attract direct
attack from vandals.
Luckily there are now
some very secure breed-
ing and hibernating sites
in the U.S. and these are
managed by the U.S. Fish
and Wildlife Service.

die as they fall from the protection
of their mothers. Add to this a lack
of sympathy for bats due to the
unfavorable mythology surrounding
them, it is not surprising that the
gray bat population has dropped by
75 percent from 1987. The good
news is that the species is now
well protected, and several of the
most important caves have been
secured, stabilizing numbers.

GREATER MOUSE-EARED BAT

Myotis myotis
Family: VESPERTILIONIDAE
Order: CHIROPTERA

STATUS: Lower risk, near threatened (IUCN), not listed by CITES. World population in low thousands. Related endangered species include Guatemalan bat (*Myotis cobanensis*) and Indiana bat (*M. sodalis*).

DISTRIBUTION: Open woodland, parkland, and old pasture in central and southern Europe south of Israel and Jordan and east to Belarus. Often roost in caves.

SIZE: Length, head and body, 2.6–3.1in (6.7-7.9cm); tail 1.8–2.4in (4.5–6cm); wingspan 13.8–17.8in (35–45cm). Weight 1–1.4oz (28–40g).

FORM: Large, short-nosed bat with broad wings and long ears, the front edges of which are curved backward. Fur, nose, and ears gray-brown. Wing membrane extends down side of body.

DIET: Mostly beetles, but also grasshoppers, spiders, and moths.

BREEDING: One young per year, born from June onward. Life span 22 years.

CONSERVATION: The greater mouse-eared bat is one of Europe's largest bats. Once found in large colonies, populations have now declined so dramatically that the bat is already extinct in parts of northern Europe. No single explanation accounts for the bat's widespread decline. Lack of suitable food due to intensive agriculture may be one cause, while timber-treatment chemicals in roofs may affect breeding. Some bats may have been deliberately killed when churches, castles, and other large buildings have been sealed up to keep bats out.

Disturbance of colonies can be another problem. The bats like to hibernate in caves, but the noise and light caused by cavers wakes them up – they then consume vital reserves of fat that they need to last them through the winter, and may die as a result.

In an attempt to stop this wide-scale decline, the species now has full legal protection in all the countries in which it still occurs. In recent years the population seems to have stabilized, and it can only be hoped that protective measures will in time bring about a recovery.

LONG-DISTANCE SURVIVORS
This bat's ability to migrate seasonally, sometimes 50 to 100 miles (80–160km) may help it recolonize parts of Europe where it once lived. Conservation work has also helped to stabilize numbers.

KITTI'S HOG-NOSED BAT

Craseonycteris thonglongyai
Family: CRASEONYCTERIDAE
Order: CHIROPTERA

THAILAND

STATUS: Endangered (IUCN), not listed by CITES. World population 2,000–2,500. Related endangered species: no close relatives, but one mouse-tailed bat (rhinopoma macinnesi) is listed, also some sheath-tailed bats and 9 other similar species.

DISTRIBUTION: Deep caves in forests of western Thailand, along the Kwai River.

SIZE: Length 1.1–1.3in (2.9–3.3cm); wingspan about 5.5in (13.5cm). Weight about 0.07oz (2g).

FORM: Minute bat with no tail; piglike snout with flattened end that is swollen around nostrils. Ears large and pointed.

DIET: Tiny insects caught in flight; spiders and insect larvae on leaves.

BREEDING: Single young born once a year between April and May. Life span unknown, but likely to be at least 5–10 years.

CONSERVATION: A tiny, shy creature that seeks refuge in the darkest recesses of limestone caves, Kitti's hog-nosed bat was only discovered in 1973. It lives only along the Kwai River in western Thailand, a region riddled with small limestone caves. An area of about 2.5 square miles (6.5 sq km) has been designated a national park where the bats are protected. The bats have been found in about two dozen caves, some outside the protected area. At one time, Kitti's hog-nosed bats hunted among the dense foliage of the tropical forest, snatching insects from the air and hovering to pick spiders and insect larvae off leaves. However, much of the forest was cleared in the 1950s to make way for farmland and teak plantations, and the bats now feed among fields of cassava or kapok, taking mostly tiny flies. They rarely fly far off the ground so they have presumably been forced to alter their feeding behavior in response to the habitat changes. The species is considered to be endangered because of its restricted range in a region that has been heavily affected by human activity. Even through their caves are now mostly protected, the animals still risk occasional disturbance from visitors eager to see the world's smallest bat species.

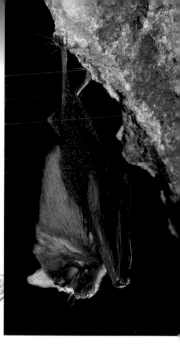

TINIEST MAMMAL IN THE WORLD
Kitti's hog-nosed bat is the size of a bumblebee. Its wings are relatively broad, which allows it to hover – an adaptation that may have helped the bats maneuver among dense foliage.

RYUKYU FLYING FOX

Pteropus dasymallus
Family: PTEROPODIDAE
Order: CHIROPTERA

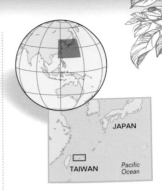

JAPAN

TAIWAN

Pacific
Ocean

STATUS: Endangered (IUCN), CITES II. A few hundred left in the world. Related endangered species include Rodrigues flying fox (*Pteropus rodricensis*) and 34 other species of *Pteropus*.

DISTRIBUTION: Forest, fruit trees of Ryukyu (Nansei) Islands, Japan.

SIZE: Length 8in (22cm); wingspan over 3ft (1m). Weight 1lb (400–450g).

FORM: Large fruit bat with typical "foxy" face and big eyes. Varies in color from pale brown to black, sometimes with pale colored collar or chest.

DIET: Variety of soft tree fruit, often swallowing only the juice but dispersing seeds and pips which aids forest growth. Also eats figs, flowers, insects, and leaves.

BREEDING: One young born per year. Life span unknown but could be 20 years.

CONSERVATION: This so-called flying fox is in fact a type of fruit-eating bat. There are five local varieties, each living on a different island. As their habitats are mostly small, the animals have probably never been very numerous. But it plays a vital role in the forest ecosystem. The undigested parts of the fruit it consumes are discarded, often miles from where the fruit was collected – this is an important mechanism for dispersing seeds of forest trees. They also feed on flowers and help pollinate them. Their protection is therefore essential to help maintain sustainable forests. Yet subspecies of the Ryukyu flying fox are threatened by loss of habitat, as trees are removed for timber, fuel, and to create farmland.

In addition, large numbers are still routinely collected for food, leaving young bats unable to fend for themselves and therefore highly vulnerable. In response, the Japanese government has given the Ryukyu flying fox legal protection. However it has not created any protected areas in which the bats can live undisturbed. Although numbers are high on some islands, forest removal is still affecting the Ryukyu group.

DAYTIME EXPOSURE
The Ryukyu flying fox likes to hang out in the open – an activity that leaves it vulnerable to the slightest disturbance and to being shot or captured. The larger bats are commonly killed for eating. Flying into overhead power cables is another cause of fatalities.

EURASIAN BEAVER

Castor fiber
Family: CASTORIDAE
Order: RODENTIA

STATUS: Lower risk, near threatened (IUCN), not listed by CITES. World population about 500,000. No close relatives that are endangered.

DISTRIBUTION: Widespread (although patchy) from France to China; Mediterranean countries north to Scandinavia, in broad river valleys, swamps, and floodplains, where trees are found beside slow-flowing water.

SIZE: Length, head and body, 30–36in (75–90cm); tail 11–16in (28–38cm). Weight up to 84lb (38kg).

FORM: Heavy body with dark fur and a broad, flattened tail. Large orange incisor teeth; small ears and eyes set near the top of the head.

DIET: Plant material, mostly grasses, leaves, and twigs.

BREEDING: One litter per year of up to 8 young (usually 4–5);

reach maturity at just under 2 years. Life span 10 years in wild; up to 25 or more in captivity.

CONSERVATION: For centuries Eurasian beavers were hunted and trapped for their fur, meat, and an oily scent the animal produces that was prized as a traditional medicine. As a result, they were driven to extinction over much of Europe. In Britain, for example, the last animals were killed before the 1500s. Thankfully, the demise of the beaver has now been halted by effective protection measures – today beavers have been restored to 13 European countries.

Although hunting is no longer a serious problem for the species, today there is a new danger in the form of road traffic. The effect of road accidents can be severe, often wiping out whole families as they move between isolated ponds. When youngsters leave their birth colony, they sometimes travel over 60 miles (100 km) to find a

new home. Inevitably the young beavers have to cross roads, and many are run over. There is also a threat from detergent pollutants in the water which may interfere with the vital insulation provided by the beaver's fur. Another potential danger is that the American beaver has now been introduced to Finland and Austria. Although the American beaver does not interbreed with the Eurasian species, the newcomers may cause difficulties by competing for food resources.

REINTRODUCTIONS
Hunting may no longer be a threat to the Eurasian beaver, but habitat loss and pollution certainly are. Reintroductions have, however, been successful in many European countries including Latvia, France, the Netherlands, and Hungary – all of which have thriving beaver populations.

JAPANESE DORMOUSE

JAPAN

Glirulus japonicus
Family: GLIRIDAE
Order: RODENTIA

STATUS: Endangered (IUCN), not listed by CITES. World population is unknown, but said to be small and declining. Related endangered species include Chinese dormouse (*Dryomys sichuanensis*) and common dormouse (*Muscardinus avellanarius*).

DISTRIBUTION: Mountain forests, generally 1,250–5,500ft (400–1,800m) above sea level, in the Japanese islands of Honshu, Kyushu, and Shikoku.

SIZE: Length, head and body, 2.5–3.2in (6.5–8cm); tail 1.6–2.2in (4–5.5cm). Weight 0.5–1.4oz (14–40g).

FORM: Pale olive or gray-brown mouse with dark stripe down middle of the back. Dense, soft fur; tail flattened and fluffy.

DIET: Fruit, flowers, insects, and occasional bird eggs. All collected among the branches of trees rather than from the ground.

BREEDING: Up to 7 young (usually 4), born June–July or later; 1 or 2 litters per year. Life span unknown, but may be about 5 years.

CONSERVATION: The Japanese dormouse, or yamane, is rarely seen and little known, mainly because it lives in an inaccessible habitat and is only active at night. It is also rare and in decline – 50 percent of its population may have been lost in the last decade. This is chiefly due to forest clearance and to the remaining patches of forest being too small to support populations. As a result, the species has been classified as endangered. To encourage the public interest in dormouse conservation, the Japanese government launched a campaign

to educate its people. It has used T-shirts, and a yamane museum where schoolchildren can watch the dormice feeding at night in the trees outside, to promote the dormouse. It has even designated it a national symbol. In addition, where areas of woodland have been isolated by roads and rail track, bridges have been made to help the dormice cross the open gaps – an attempt to prevent inbreeding which weakens the species.

GOVERNMENT BACKED RODENT
The Japanese dormouse, or yamane as it is also called, is rare, but recent publicity and educational campaigns in Japan have succeeded in making it a widely appreciated national treasure.

SHORT-TAILED CHINCHILLA

Chinchilla brevicaudata
Family: CHINCHILLIDAE
Order: RODENTIA

STATUS: Critical (IUCN); CITES I. Population unknown; possibly extinct in the wild; some may have survived in remote areas. Related endangered species: Long-tailed chinchilla *(Chinchilla lanigera)*.

DISTRIBUTION: Burrows or crevices on rocky mountain slopes at 9,800–16,400ft (3,000–5,000m) above sea level in northern Argentina, Bolivia, northern Chile, and southern Peru.

SIZE: Length head/body 8.5–15in (22–38cm); tail 2.7–5.8in (7–15cm); female up to 80 percent larger than the male. Weight 14–28oz (400–800g).

FORM: Rabbit-sized, bushy-tailed rodent with incredibly dense, silky-soft gray fur; tail has a dark streak along its length. Large black eyes, and large rounded ears.

DIET: Almost any plant material: seeds, fruit, grain, herbs, and mosses.

BREEDING: Two or 3 litters of 1–6 (usually 1 or 2) young born May–November after 4-month gestation; weaned at 6 weeks; mature at about 8 months. Life span up to 10 years in the wild.

CONSERVATION: You need only to touch the short-tailed chinchilla's bluish-gray coat to understand why this species is endangered. Chinchillas have what is widely considered the softest, finest fur of any mammal. These rodents have been highly prized since the Incas ruled Peru from the 1100s. They mostly hunted chinchillas for their meat. However, when Europeans settled in the region after the Spanish conquest of 1532, they trapped the short-tailed chinchillas for their fur. By 1910, the chinchilla

population had fallen so low that trapping was banned. The potential for farmed chinchillas later emerged and millions now live in captivity on fur farms or as pets. Attempts to release chinchillas into the wild have to date failed. Animals whose survival instincts have been diluted by domestication do not fare well in the wild. Though it is over 50 years since the last sightings, some of these chinchillas may survive in remote parts of their South American habitat.

EXTINCT IN THE WILD?
The short-tailed chinchilla was last confirmed to be living in the wild in 1953, although there were reports of some of these rodents living in Lauca National Park in Chile in 1970.

AMAMI RABBIT

Pentalagus furnessi
Family: LEPORIDAE
Order: LAGOMORPHA

STATUS: Endangered (IUCN); not listed by CITES. About 2,500 exist, spread across 2 islands. Related endangered species: Volcano rabbit *(Romerolagus diazi)*; hispid hare *(Caprolagus hispidis)*; bushman hare *(Bunolagus monticularis)*; Sumatran hare *(Nesolagus netscheri)*.

DISTRIBUTION: Dense, temperate forests in Japan – only on two of the Ryukyu Islands (Amami Oshima and Tokuno-shima).

SIZE: Length 17–20in (43–51cm). Weight 4.4–6.6lb (2–3kg).

FORM: Medium-sized, thickset, with warm-brown, almost black fur. Both ears and legs are short.

DIET: Leaves and shoots, especially bamboo, pampas grass, and sweet potato; also acorns and some berries.

BREEDING: Two litters of 2 or 3 young born each year in

RELIANCE ON HUMANS
Amami rabbits need both the help of forest managers and members of the public if they are to survive. Reductions in the populations of feral cats and mongoose, which are a threat to them, are vital.

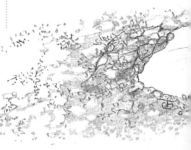

underground burrow. Average life span is probably about 1 year.

CONSERVATION: Large areas of the dense, temperate forest where this shy creature lives have been felled, the timber being used for making wood pulp. Mature forest is vital to the Amami rabbit's survival, not only because it offers cover, but also winter food. Once an area has been cleared, it will be at least a decade before new trees produce enough acorns to support even a few rabbits. A more recent threat was the building of new roads that effectively isolated populations of rabbits living on two peninsulas. These populations are thought to have since died out. To increase the species' chances of survival, trees must be taken down in small, scattered areas to create clearings where important rabbit foods like bamboo and pampas grass can flourish, but without destroying the trees that provide cover and high-energy winter foods.

STEPPE PIKA

Ochotona pusilla
Family: OCHOTONIDAE
Order: LAGOMORPHA

STATUS: Vulnerable (IUCN), not listed by CITES. Unknown world population, but declining rapidly. Related endangered species: Helan Shan pika (*Ochonota helenshanensis*), Koslov's pika (*O. koslowi*).

DISTRIBUTION: Open plains, deserts, and dry grassland steppes of Russia and Kazakhstan, between Volga and Irtysh Rivers.

SIZE: Length: 5–12in (12.5–30cm). Weight: 4.5–14oz (125–400g).

FORM: Dumpy, grayish-brown animal resembling small, round-eared rabbit with no visible tail and short legs; thick, dense fur.

DIET: Plant material, including leaves of grasses, sedges, and herbs; also twigs and flowers of woody plants.

BREEDING: Between 3 and 5 litters of 3–13 young born throughout spring and summer.

Gestation period is about 1 month. Life span can be more than 5 years in the wild.

CONSERVATION: The decline of the steppe pika dates back to the the Middle Ages. Changes in land use then drove the steppe pika out of large parts of their former range in what is now the Ukraine. The western part of the pika's range continued to be eroded, and by the early 19th century there were no pikas west of the Volga River. The remaining populations are fragmented and are at risk of being poisoned, snared, or shot. Their habitat is disappearing under farmland, leaving the pikas little choice but to raid crops, provoking the hatred of farmers and plantation owners.

The saplings of conifer plantations make easy winter pickings, when the trees are buried in snow and the pikas can feed unseen. The trees then die, and the frustration of landowners on finding their crops ruined is understandable.

LONG-TERM DECLINE
Steppe pikas compete with humans for a living on the steppes. While this situation continues, the pika's future will be at risk.

AQUATIC TENREC

Limnogale mergulus
Family: TENRECIDAE
Order: INSECTIVORA

STATUS: Endangered (IUCN); not listed by CITES. Unknown world population. Related endangered species: Giant otter shrew *(Potamogale velox)*; Ruwenzori otter shrew *(Micropotamogale ruwenzorii)*; Mount Nimba otter shrew *(M. lamottei)*; 6 species of long-tailed tenrec *(Microgale spp.)*.

DISTRIBUTION: Clean, fast-flowing rivers and streams at 2,000–4,000ft (600–1,200m) in scattered sites on eastern Madagascar in the Indian Ocean.

SIZE: Length head/body: 4.5–6.5in (12–17cm). Weight: 2–3oz (60–90g).

FORM: Large ratlike animal with soft, dense, brown fur and gray belly; eyes and ears small and inconspicuous; feet webbed; tail slightly flattened and with fringe of stiff hairs.

MADAGASCAR

FAST FLOWING FUR
The rarest of the tenrec family, the aquatic tenrec needs fast-flowing rivers for hunting and to keep its fur in optimum condition.

DIET: Frogs, fish, aquatic crustaceans, and insect larvae
.

BREEDING: Little is known; litters of 1–6 young are born from December to January.

CONSERVATION: The aquatic tenrec is extremely rare and apparently restricted to a few scattered sites in and around the Eanomafana National Park in eastern Madagascar. Few live specimens have been recorded, but concerted efforts are being made to find out more about these threatened animals. Financial resources for such research are difficult to find, not least because Madagascar itself is a poor country.

Captive breeding is not a realistic option for the species. Exporting tenrecs from Madagascar to zoos elsewhere in the world would be problematic, since every tenrec that died or failed to breed would simply add to the crisis facing the species as a whole. In its natural habitat, these tenrecs are extremely sensitive to even minor changes or attempts to create an artificial site. For example, in the wild aquatic tenrecs live in burrows on the banks of fast-flowing rivers and streams from which they emerge to hunt at night. Fast-flowing water is crucial to its survival, since it continually rinses and conditions the animal's fur. Slow-moving or stagnant water would allow the fur to become fouled, and lose its waterproofing and insulating properties. Changes in water flow may also affect availability of prey.

CUBAN SOLENODON

Solenodon cubanos
Family: SOLENODONTIDAE
Order: INSECTIVORA

STATUS: Endangered (IUCN); not listed by CITES. Population probably low hundreds. Related endangered species: Haitian solenodon (*Solenodon paradoxus*).

DISTRIBUTION: Dense jungles, thick scrub, and areas around the plantations of eastern Cuba.

SIZE: Length head/body: 11–13in (28–32cm); tail 7–10in (17–25cm). Weight: about 1.5–2.2lb (0.7–1kg).

FORM: Resembles giant shrew with long, pointed snout and long, bare tail. Usually dark brown or blackish. Five toes on each foot; prominent claws on toes. Grooved lower incisor tooth carries toxic saliva to the prey when bitten.

DIET: Roots around in leaf litter with long snout, mainly for insects, grubs, worms and small animals (lizards and spiders).

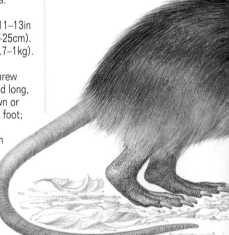

BREEDING: One or 2 young per litter; the young stay with the mother for several months (a long time for an insectivore). May live up to 6 years.

CONSERVATION: Cuban solenodons have only a few young at a time, with long periods in between. As a result, they cannot withstand heavy losses. European settlers in Cuba introduced cats, dogs, and mongoose to control rats in the sugar plantations and solenodons were caught in large numbers. Their forest habitats were converted into farms, with open fields making the creatures even more vulnerable. By the 1960s the Cuban species was believed to be extinct, but surveys in the 1970s located some living specimens, and it was concluded that they were probably widely distributed in certain parts of eastern Cuba, where the human population is comparatively low. The animal has no economic, medicinal or nutritional value, so it has not been hunted, and now has full legal protection. It is hoped that it will benefit from protected highland areas that have been specially set aside for conservation.

PROTECTION AGAINST PREDATORS
The Cuban solenodon is a relatively slow-moving animal that seems to walk with a drunken stagger. Although it can climb well, it is not able to jump, so it is easy game for predators, such as dogs.

GIANT OTTER SHREW

Potamogale velox
Family: TENRECIDAE
Order: INSECTIVORA

STATUS: Endangered (IUCN); not
listed by CITES Population
unknown. Related endangered
species: Nimba otter shrew
(*Micdropotamogale*); pygmy otter
shrew (*M. ruwenzorii*); aquatic
tenrec (*Limnogale mergulus*).

DISTRIBUTION: Fast- and slow-
moving streams from sea level to
5,900ft (1,800m) in 12 countries in
central Africa, including Nigeria,
Gabon and Cameroon.

SIZE: Length head/body:
11.5–14in (29–35cm); tail: 9.5–35in
(24.5–90cm). Weight: 12–14oz
(340–400g).

FORM: Otterlike animal with
cylindrical body, powerful tail, and
short legs; fur short and dense,
brown to black above, pale below;
head has broad, flat snout with stiff
whiskers, small eyes and ears.

DIET: Freshwater crustaceans
(mainly crabs); also mollusks, fish,
insects, and amphibians.

BREEDING: Two litters of 1 or 2
young born at any time of year.

CONSERVATION: Although it is
trapped for its silky fur, the decline
in the numbers of the giant otter
shrew probably has more to do

HUNTED FOR FUR
The giant otter shrew has fine, dense fur that traps an insulating layer of air, giving it a silvery appearance under water. It has been hunted for its pelt (fur) in many parts of its central African range.

with habitat destruction than hunting. The animals live in streams that pass through forested areas. They do not venture far from the water, and it is possible that they could survive with only a narrow strip of trees on either side of the water course. It would certainly cost the timber companies little to leave such areas alone when they cut down the rest of the forest. A side effect of deforestation is a dramatic increase in soil erosion. Soil and silt – no longer bound up by tree roots or protected and enriched by a layer of humus – are washed into streams and rivers every time it rains. In the wet season, especially, streams become muddy torrents that contaminate habitats normally suitable for otter shrews. They can only hunt successfully if there is plenty of prey around. With mud and silt

blocking out the sunlight, few aquatic plants can grow, so plant-eating stream creatures that are the otter shrews' prey are scarce. The gills and filter-feeding mechanisms of fish and crustaceans become clogged, and they soon die off, leaving the otter shrew with nothing to eat. There are no otter shrews in captivity, and nobody knows how many survive in the wild; the rapid destruction of their habitat by local and upstream deforestation means that they are facing a serious decline.

HAINAN GYMNURE

Hylomys hainanensis
Family: ERINACEIDAE
Order: INSECTIVORA

STATUS: Endangered (IUCN); not listed by CITES. Population unknown. Related endangered species: Dwarf gymnure *(Hylomys parvus)*; Dinagat moonrat *(Podogymnura aureospinula)*; Mindanao gymnure *(P.truei)*.

DISTRIBUTION: Dense forests on Hainan Island, China.

SIZE: Length head/body: 4.8–5.8in (12–15cm); tail: 1.5–1.8in (3.5–4.5cm). Weight: 1.8–2.5oz (50–70g).

FORM: Rat-sized animal with pointed snout and bare, scaly tail; brown body with black stripe down the back.

DIET: Insects, worms, and other invertebrates. Can climb trees to search for birds' nests and other food sources.

BREEDING: Poorly known; probably 2–5 young born once or twice per year. Life span of 5 years likely.

CONSERVATION: Resembling a furry hedgehog, the exact status of this flat-footed creature is difficult to determine because it is so elusive. Hidden in dense

tropical forests, often on steep mountainsides where it is hard to find, the animal is seriously threatened, if only because of its restricted distribution. Hainan Island is only 150 miles (240km) in diameter, so the land area available is limited. The island is also overcrowded and most of the island's forest cover has been removed, and the rest is under constant threat. Within the forest the dense tree canopy stays green all year round, casting shade which keeps the ground moist. Once

trees are removed, the soil dries, reducing the number of invertebrates on which the Hainan gymnure can feed. Opening up the habitat also exposes the animal to predators such as dogs and birds of prey. Wildlife reserves have been established, but they are hard to protect, and the distribution of gymnures within them is unknown. If forest clearance continues at the current rate, it is easily possible that the species may disappear during the next 50 years.

FURRY HEDGEHOG
A little-known relative of the hedgehog, the Hainan Gymnure has dense fur in place of spines. It is not hunted, but the species is threatened by the loss of the forest habitat on which it depends.

RUSSIAN DESMAN

Desmana moschata
Family: TALPIDAE
Order: INSECTIVORA

STATUS: Vulnerable (IUCN); not listed by CITES. About 40,000 remain. Related endangered species: Pyrenean desman (*Galemys pyrenaicus*).

DISTRIBUTION: Permanently wet habitats, such as lakes, marshes, and the river systems of the Don, Ural, and Volga in southwestern Russia and the Ukraine.

SIZE: Length head/body: 7–9in (18–22cm); tail: 7–8.5in (17–21.5cm). Weight: 1.75–3.5oz (50–100g).

FORM: Ratlike mammal with long, flexible nose and long, glossy hair. Tail scaly and flattened; partially webbed feet. Various parts of the body have sensory whiskers.

DIET: Aquatic insects, mollusks, fish, and frogs.

BREEDING: Families of 3–5 young produced twice per year. Life span unknown, probably 2–3 years.

CONSERVATION: Like mink and muskrats, desmans have a coat that has dense, soft underfur and long, glossy "guard" hairs. This two-layer coat effectively insulates the animals from the cold water, but also provides a superb fur for the fashion industry.

The Russian desman was extensively hunted with traps in the 19th century, but when it was officially recognized as rare in

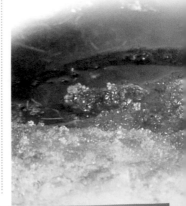

1929, and given legal protection, most trapping ended. However, other threats loomed. Hydroelectric projects affected water flow and therefore the suitability of the habitat for both the desman and its diet of water-dwelling invertebrates. In addition, grazing farm animals and riverside development removed the vegetation from the river banks, taking away the places where the desmans build their burrows. A further threat has come from introduced rodents that are kept on fur farms and then released or have escaped into the desman's home waters. Water quality, affected by industrial and agricultural pollution, has also impacted on the species. The influx of nutrients encourages the growth of algae, which multiply, using all the oxygen; this kills insects and crustaceans, the desmans' main food. Conservationists have now captured and released over 10,000 Russian desmans into places where competition and pollution threats are less serious.

POOR WATER QUALITY
The Russian desman has suffered as a result of water pollution and from competition with introduced species. To counter this, thousands have been released into special refuges to protect the populations, but numbers are still declining.

GIANT ARMADILLO

Priodontes maximus
Family: DASYPODIDAE
Order: XENARTHRA

STATUS: Endangered (IUCN);
CITES I. Population unknown;
perhaps low thousands. Related
endangered species: Fairy
armadillo *(Chlamyphorus
truncatus)*; hairy armadillo
(Chaetophractus retusus);
Brazilian three-banded armadillo
(Tolypeutes tricinctus).

DISTRIBUTION: Forests and
scrubland in South America, from
Venezuela to northeastern
Argentina.

SIZE: Length head/body: 30–39in
(75–100cm); tail: 18–20in
(45–50cm). Weight: 99–132lb
(45–60kg).

FORM: Bulky, dark-brown animal
with long tail; head, back, and hips
covered by rows of small, bony,
horn-covered plates. Elsewhere
skin covered with stiff hair. Snout
slightly elongated with long, flexible
tongue; eyes and ears small. Front
feet have long, curved claws which
are good digging tools.

DIET: Termites; ants and other
insects; worms, spiders, snails, and
small snakes; some carrion.

BREEDING: One, sometimes
2 young born after 4-month
gestation; weaned at 4–6 weeks;
mature at 9–12 months. May live
up to 15 years in the wild.

CONSERVATION: The armadillo has
few natural enemies, and its size
and body armor equip it well
against potential predators such as
the jaguar. Because of its solitary
lifestyle, it needs large areas of
habitat. These are being destroyed

by logging, by the spread of towns and agriculture, and by the flooding of large areas of rain forest to create reservoirs. Salvation may lie in the fact that armadillos are the only known animal hosts of leprosy. The armadillo may become a model for scientists in their efforts to find an effective treatment.

ARMOR-PLATED HIDE
The giant armadillo may be protected from predators by its "armor", but this cannot save it from human activity, such as logging.

GIANT ANTEATER

Myrmecophaga tridactyla
Family: MYRMECOPHAGIDAE
Order: XENARTHRA

STATUS: Vulnerable (IUCN); CITES II. Unknown population; probably low thousands.

DISTRIBUTION: Low-lying grasslands and open forests in Central and South America, from southern Belize and Guatemala to northern Argentina, with populations in Brazil, Colombia, Costa Rica, French Guiana, Peru, Paraguay, and Venezuela.

HUNTERS' TROPHY
The giant anteater is in decline but not yet at the brink of extinction. However, unless steps are taken to secure its grassland and open forest habitats, the future of the animal will be in crisis.

SIZE: Length head/body: 39–47in (100–120cm); tail: 26–36in (65–90cm); males 10–20% bigger than females. Weight: 39–86lb (18–39kg).

FORM: Bulky body; tapered, narrow snout. Gray-brown fur, long on legs and tail; white-bordered dark band tapers from chest to flank over each shoulder. Eyes and ears small. Long, narrow tongue can be extended up to 24in (60cm).

DIET: Ants, termites and their eggs, grubs, and cocoons; beetle larvae and fruit.

BREEDING: Single young born at any time of year after gestation of 6–7 months; fully weaned at 6 months, but may remain with mother for up to 2 years; mature at 3 years. Such a breeding rate is slow, and there is a long period of care for the young, so populations take a long time to recover from losses. In captivity, a life span of up to 26 years is possible.

CONSERVATION: The anteater's long claws and hugely powerful forelegs are formidable weapons against attack by jaguars or pumas. This armory is no match for a gun, however, and unregulated trophy hunting has had a significant impact upon the population. The anteater's claws are so long that it has to walk on its knuckles, and so cannot run fast. This lack of speed makes them vulnerable not only to hunters but to forest fires.

The giant anteater depends on large areas of undisturbed habitat with plenty of food. Plowing for crops destroys ant colonies, the major food supply, and so within their range, anteater populations have become small and thinly spread, a worrying development.

PHILIPPINE FLYING LEMUR

Cynocephalus volans
Family: CYNOCEPHALIDAE
Order: DERMOPTERA

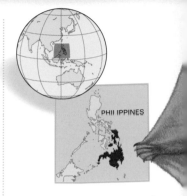

STATUS: Vulnerable (IUCN); not listed by CITES. Unknown population. Related endangered species: The Malayan colugo (*Cynocephalus variegatus*) is becoming less common but is not currently considered at risk.

DISTRIBUTION: Forests dominated by trees with few lower branches on the Philippine islands of Mindanao, Basilan, Samar, Leyte, and Bohol.

SIZE: Length head/body: 13–15in (33–38cm); tail: 8–11in (22–27cm); females are slightly larger than males. Weight: 2–3.5lb (1–1.5kg).

FORM: Females have grayish fur, males slightly reddish; both have mottling on back, providing excellent camouflage on tree bark. Limbs and tail are connected by a web of skin (the patagium); fingers and toes are also webbed and bear long, curved claws. The head is small, and the face pointed, and the eyes are large and round.

DIET: Leaves, buds, flowers, and fruit of forests and plantations.

BREEDING: A single under-developed young is born into a fold of the tail membrane after a 2-month gestation. Lifespan is unknown.

CONSERVATION: These graceful acrobats are completely dependent on the availability of the right kind of habitat – namely mature tropical forest with trees whose branches start high up the trunk. This allows an unobstructed glide path and clear areas of trunk on which to land. Over huge areas of the flying lemur's habitat, natural forest has been cleared for timber and agriculture, and replaced with

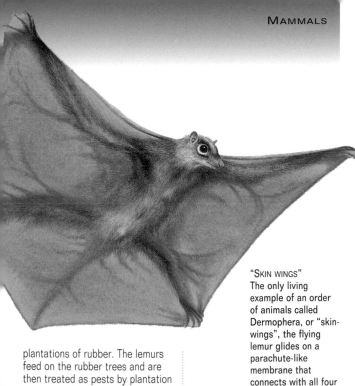

"SKIN WINGS"
The only living example of an order of animals called Dermophera, or "skin-wings", the flying lemur glides on a parachute-like membrane that connects with all four limbs and tail.

plantations of rubber. The lemurs feed on the rubber trees and are then treated as pests by plantation owners, and killed. It appears that lemur breeding rates are high, so there is good reason to suppose that they are able to build up their numbers quite quickly if given the opportunity. Increasing population sizes is urgent in the case of the Philippine flying lemur. They are not social animals and live at fairly low density, so small pockets of woodland or isolated trees are

inadequate for sustaining these amazing animals. Ensuring the Philippine flying lemur's survival will mean designating large areas of suitable forest as sanctuaries in which logging and hunting are strictly regulated, or the world may lose this very special creature.

AMAZON RIVER DOLPHIN

Inia geoffrensis
Family: INIIDAE
Order: CETACEA

STATUS: Vulnerable (IUCN);
CITES II. Unknown population
Related endangered species:
Yangtze river dolphin (*Lipotes vexillifer*); Ganges river dolphin
(*Platanista gangetica*); Indus river
dolphin (*P. minor*).

DISTRIBUTION: Orinoco and
Amazon river systems, and flooded
forests, South America.

SIZE: Length: 5.6–10ft (1.7–3m).
Weight: up to 350lb (160kg); males
can be twice as heavy.

FORM: Large, bluish-gray to pink
dolphin with long dorsal (back)
ridge and large fins and tail flukes;
small eyes, long snout and peglike
teeth, bulging cheeks and forehead.

DIET: Mostly fish; some
crustaceans and turtles.

BREEDING: Single calf born
May– September after gestation of
10–11 months; weaned at 1 year
or more.

CONSERVATION: Every year the
dolphins' river habitats flood.
When the waters subside again, the
dolphins become trapped, at least
until the rains the following year.
The dolphins usually manage to
survive a season or two in quite
small lakes, as long as there are
plenty of fish trapped along with
them. Problems arise when the
lakes are drained to irrigate crops,
or if humans compete for the same
fish prey as the dolphins. Once the
fish in the lake have all been taken,
no more can arrive to replace them
until the floods come again the
following year.

The building of dams for hydroelectric power and flood control create permanent barriers to the dolphins' passage, cutting off whole populations. Isolated groups can become inbred and vulnerable to disease and local disasters from which there is no escape either up- or downstream. Mercury poisoning is another danger to the dolphins. Mercury is used to refine the gold that is mined in the Amazon region, and hundred of tons pour into the river yearly. Mercury combines with other chemicals to produce a compound called methyl mercury, quantities of which build up in the bodies of river fish. The dolphins may eat enough of the contaminated fish to ingest sufficient methyl mercury to cause serious damage, including birth deformities, muscle-wasting, nerve damage, and failure of the immune system. If the dolphins don't die from this, or drown after being caught up in fishermen's nets, they may live to 30 years or more.

RIVER DANGERS

The amazon river dolphin, or boto, has an unusual pink skin that becomes more pronounced in color after activity. The dolphin makes its home in the Amazon, the world's largest river system, where pollution, dam-building, and overfishing are all threatening its future.

BLUE WHALE

Balaenoptera musculus
Family: BALAENIDAE
Order: CETACEA

STATUS: Endangered (IUCN), though some populations listed as Vulnerable or Lower Risk; CITES I. About 3,500 remain. Related endangered species: Fin whale (*Balanoptera physalus*); sei whale (*B. borealis*); minke whale (*B. acutorostrata*).

DISTRIBUTION: Three separate populations live deep in the North Atlantic, North Pacific, and Southern Ocean respectively; the whales migrate annually between polar and tropical waters.

SIZE: Length: 79–89ft (24–27m); occasionally up to 110ft (33m). Weight: 110–132 tons (100–120 tonnes); occasionally up to 209 tons (190 tonnes).

FORM: Vast, streamlined body; bluish-gray skin with pale markings and white to yellow underside. Rounded snout; deep throat furrows; 2 blowholes with large splashguard; small dorsal fin set well back on body.

DIET: Krill (planktonic shrimps) and other crustaceans.

BREEDING: Single young born after gestation of 10–12 months; weaned at 7–8 months; mature at 10 years. May live up to 110 years.

CONSERVATION: Advances in whaling techniques meant that by the 1960s, the blue whale was heading for extinction. An international ban on whaling was agreed but, in spite of a slight increase in numbers in the 1980s, it is now thought that the world population may be as low as 3,500.

The main reason is because their habitat has altered for the worse. The annual catch of krill taken by the world's fisheries is now so high there may not be enough food to meet the whales' daily needs. The seas are also polluted with toxins and biologically active substances that almost certainly affect large whales. Whales are also affected by noise pollution, and by alterations in local currents brought about by coastal developments. Inland projects can result in silt being dumped in the sea, making the water unsuitable for both whales and their food.

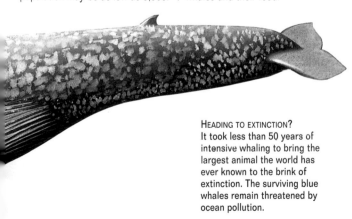

HEADING TO EXTINCTION?
It took less than 50 years of intensive whaling to bring the largest animal the world has ever known to the brink of extinction. The surviving blue whales remain threatened by ocean pollution.

Northern Right Whale

Eubalaena glacialis
Family: BALAENIDAE
Order: CETACEA

STATUS: Endangered (IUCN); CITES I. About 320 remain. Related endangered species: Southern right whale *(Eubalaena australis)*.

DISTRIBUTION: Coastal temperate regions of the North Atlantic Ocean. North Pacific right whales may be a different species.

SIZE: Length: 40–55ft (13.6–18m); females slightly larger than males. Weight: 22–112 tons (20–102 tonnes).

FORM: Large black whale with long, tapering body; no dorsal fin; huge mouth with arched upper jaw; head has barnacle-encrusted skin callouses.

DIET: Planktonic crustaceans.

BREEDING: Single calf born every 2–5 years after 13-month gestation; weaned at 7 months. Adulthood reached at 9 years.

CONSERVATION: The most endangered of all the large whales, the species' name describes the main reason: for centuries the animal was known to whalers as the "right whale" to hunt. It lived close to the shore, fed near the surface, was easy to approach by boat, and floated when dead. A single carcass

MOST HUNTED WHALE
Northern right whales may die out in under 200 years, at the current rate of decline. Intensive conservation is needed to halt the damage inflicted by 1,000 years of unregulated hunting.

could yield several hundred barrels of oil and its long, thin baleen (whalebone) plates were considered to be of the finest quality. In the space of about 10 years in the mid-19th century, the northern right whale was hunted to virtual extinction. Although it has been protected by international agreement since 1937, the northern right whale population has barely increased. Some are accidentally killed by boats plowing into them as they feed in busy shipping lanes, others are killed by fishing nets and tackle. The average birthrate of

right whales is dropping. Pollution may be one reason: coastal waters are vulnerable to this, especially industrial effluent. The decline in birthrate may be partly due to pollutants called endocrine disrupters, which interfere with normal bodily functions. Another explanation may be inbreeding due to the small size of remaining populations. Changing weather patterns in the North Atlantic have led to a decrease in marine plankton, the whales' main food.

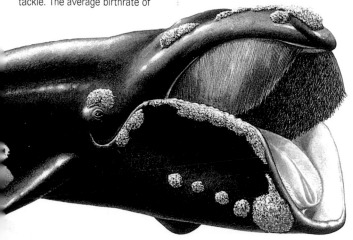

KILLER WHALE

Orcinus orca
Family: DELPHINIDAE
Order: CETACEA

STATUS: Lower Risk (IUCN); CITES II. At least 100,000 exist worldwide. Related endangered species: Hector's dolphin (*Cephalorhynchus hectori*); short-finned pilot whale (*Globiocephala macrorhynchus*); pantropical spotted dolphin (*Stenella attenuata*); striped dolphin (*S. coeruleoalba*).

DISTRIBUTION: Seas and oceans; generally in deep water, but often hunts close to shore.

SIZE: Length: 18–33ft (5.5–10m); males can be almost twice as long as females. Weight: 3–10 tons (2.5–9 tonnes).

FORM: Robust, jet-black body, with bright white chin, belly, and eye patch; gray saddle; dorsal fin tall, especially in males; pectoral fins large and paddle shaped.

DIET: Fish, squid, seals, sea lions, turtles, and seabirds; also small whales and dolphins.

BREEDING: Single young born at any time of year after 17-month gestation; weaned at 14–18 months; mature at 12–16 years. Males may live up to 60 years, females up to 90 years.

CONSERVATION: Also called orcas, killer whales have never been a principal catch for whalers, but whaling crews whose main target was the larger baleen whales would also take orcas if they came across them. Hunting reached a peak in 1979–80, when whalers from the Soviet Union alone killed over 900 orcas in the Southern Ocean. Fishermen also kill them to preserve their fish stocks.

Being at the top of the marine food chain means that killer whales are at risk of exposure to heavy accumulations of chemical contaminants in the flesh of their prey. Pesticides, fertilizers, sewage, and effluents contain potentially harmful compounds.

KILLER KILLED
Killer whales, the
world's largest
predators of
mammals and birds,
are not man-eaters
by nature. In the
vast majority of
encounters with
humans it has been
people that have
done the killing.

However, no one knows just
how damaging these industrial
by-products might be.
Several hundred orcas have
been captured live and taken to
marine parks, where they are
trained to perform tricks. Such
exhibitions have revealed the killer
whale's playful nature. While the
species has grown in public
affection, it has also raised
awareness of the morality of
hunting them or of keeping them in
captivity. Keiko, an orca who
starred in the film *Free Willy*, came
to symbolize the whole issue of
cetaceans in captivity.

HARBOR PORPOISE

Phocoena phocoena
Family: PHOCOENIDAE
Order: CETACAE

STATUS: Vulnerable (IUCN); CITES II. About 250,000 remain. Related endangered species: Gulf of California porpoise (*Phocoena sinus*); Burmeister's porpoise (*P. spinipinnis*).

DISTRIBUTION: Shallow coasts and estuaries in the cool temperate waters of the North Atlantic, North Pacific, Arctic; isolated population in the Black Sea.

SIZE: Length: 4–6ft (120–190cm). Weight: 100–132lb (45–60kg); up to 198lb (90kg).

FORM: Stout, with blunt, conical snout; dark gray skin above, fading to almost white on belly.

DIET: Schooling fish (cod, pollack, herring, hake, salmon, and sardines); also squid and shrimps.

BREEDING: Single calf born May–August after 11-month gestation; weaned at 8 months. Life span up to 14 years.

NET EFFECT
A shy animal, the harbor porpoise is less acrobatic than most dolphins but is highly intelligent, and deserving of all conservation efforts to prevent further loss of numbers caught accidentally in fishermen's nets.

CONSERVATION: Porpoise numbers underwent a dramatic decline in the 20th century, and some populations, in the Mediterranean for example, are virtually extinct. The loss of harbor porpoises from the Mediterranean means that the population in the Black Sea is now extremely isolated. Elsewhere, intensive hunting and accidental killing by the United States, Canada, and especially Danish fisheries inflict a death toll somewhere in the region of 10,000 porpoises per year. Harbor porpoises have another enemy in the form of the bottlenosed dolphin – fatal wounding is not uncommon. The full reasons for this unusual aggression between species are not yet understood. Porpoises also frequently fall prey to sharks – such natural hazards are a possible reason for the porpoise's shyness.

There is evidence that porpoises are also being regularly affected by pollution and disease. International restrictions on hunting would certainly help the harbor porpoise, but further action is needed to prevent accidents caused by fishing nets and tackle, which kill thousands of porpoises a year. For example, nets could be equipped with acoustic "pingers" to warn the porpoises away.

MEDITERRANEAN MONK SEAL

Monachus monachus
Family: PHOCIDAE
Order: CARNIVORA

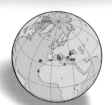

STATUS: Critical (IUCN); CITES I. About 500 remain. Related endangered species: Hawaiian monk seal (*Monachus shauinslandi*); Caribbean monk seal (*M. tropicalis*).

DISTRIBUTION: Scattered populations live on sheltered subtropical coast, beaches, and sea caves around the Mediterranean and on the Atlantic coast of Mauritania in northwestern Africa.

SIZE: Length: 7.5–9.2ft (2.3–2.8m). Weight: 550–660lb (250–300kg).

FORM: Large seal with short, dark, variably patterned coat; pale patch on belly.

DIET: Fish, octopus, and squid.

BREEDING: Single pup born May–November after gestation of 9–10 months; weaned at 6 weeks but stays with mother for 3 years; mature at 4 years. May live up to 23 years.

CONSERVATION: It is largely as a result of centuries of hunting and habitat disturbance that the Mediterranean monk seal is now one of the world's rarest mammals. The main hazard facing Mediterranean monk seal populations today comes from the region's fishing and tourism industries. These seals once used to pup on wide, sandy beaches. Today, the same beaches are lined with hotels and visited by sunbathers and yachts. The sensitive seals now rarely breed away from secluded coves surrounded by high cliffs, which are inaccessible to people. Most seals choose the even greater security of sea caves that can only be reached by underwater entrance tunnels. Pregnant females are especially sensitive to disturbance, and fairly minor incidents can cause them to miscarry.They rarely have more than one pup every year, and the overall reproduction rate is relatively slow. Another serious

UNDER PRESSURE
The Mediterranean monk seal remains under pressure from tourism as it tries to find undisturbed beaches on which have its pups.

problem is competition with Mediterranean fishermen. This sea is one of the most intensively fished areas in the world. Humans and seals have similar tastes in seafood and the seals regularly become entangled in fishing nets. Unable to return to the surface to breathe, they drown in minutes. Efforts to save the seal require determined international cooperation. An intensive program of education, along with compensation for fishermen, should mean that persecution is a thing of the past. However, even with protection, populations are now so small that they are increasingly vulnerable to natural hazards. Until the Mediterranean monk seal population is large enough to survive these incidents, it will remain one of the world's most critically endangered species.

STELLER'S SEA COW

Hydrodamalis gigas
Family: DUGONGIDAE
Order: SIRENIA

RUSSIA

Pacific Ocean

STATUS: Extinct (IUCN); not listed by CITES. Related endangered species: Dugong *(Dugong dugon)*; Amazon manatee *(Trichechus inunguis)*; American manatees *(T. manatus –* includes Florida manatee *T. manatus latirostris)*; African manatee *(T. senegalensis)*.

DISTRIBUTION: Along the coast of the Commander (Komandorskiye) and Aleutian Islands in the Bering Sea, North Pacific Ocean. Fossil evidence from California.

SIZE: Total length of a female, probably the only one ever measured: 24.6ft (7.5m); circumference of body: 20.3ft (6.2m); probably grew larger sometimes. Weight: probably up to 11 tons (10 tonnes).

FORM: A large, whalelike animal with small, blunt head and forked tail flipper. Forelimbs formed paddles; no hind limbs. Skin thick and brown, sometimes blotchy. Sparse, bristly hairs.

DIET: Various seaweeds.

BREEDING: Probably only 1 young at long intervals. Life span unknown, but likely to have been at least 20 years.

CONSERVATION: The sea cow was a close relative of today's manatees and dugongs, and it lived in the North Pacific. It was discovered in 1741 by an expedition, led by the Danish explorer Vitus Bering, that was shipwrecked off Siberia. The crew killed sea cows to provide food for their survival. There may have been as many as 2,000 sea cows at this time. However, this represented the dying remnants of what had once been a much more widespread species.

The animals moved
slowly in the water,
surfacing to breathe air.
This made them easy to
approach and snare with a hook
on a long rope. The sea cow's
reproduction rate was too slow to
compensate for the loss of life, and
by 1768 the species had been
wiped out.

WIPED OUT
In just 30 years
humans managed to
hunt this sea mammal
to extinction.

DUGONG

Dugong dugon
Family: DUGONGIDAE
Order: SIRENIA

STATUS: Vulnerable (IUCN); CITES II (Australian population); elsewhere CITES I. Fewer than 150,000 remain. No close living relatives but 3 species of manatee are listed as Vulnerable.

DISTRIBUTION: Shallow seas off coasts of Indian and southwestern Pacific oceans.

SIZE: Length head to tail: 8–9ft (2.4–2.7m), occasionally up to 13ft (4m) Weight: 300–800lb (230–360kg), occasionally up to 2,000lb (900kg).

FORM: Large, superficially sealike mammal with tough, gray, almost hairless hide, jointed front flippers, and broad, flat tail. Small eyes and large upper lip with tough, bristly pads.

DIET: Grazes on sea grasses and grubs up nutritional roots using its upper lip at the end of its broad snout; occasionally eats green and brown seaweed.

BREEDING: Single young (rarely twins) born every 3–7 years at any time of year, after gestation of 13–14 months. Young first graze at 3 months; fully weaned at 18 months; mature at 9–10 years. Life span up to 73 years.

CONSERVATION: The graceful, gentle dugong is the only living species in its family. Its closest relative, Steller's sea cow, was hunted to extinction in the 18th century. At one time dugongs were common around the edges of the tropical oceans. However, they have been hunted for their meat, oil, and their thick hides, which produce good leather. Dugongs are mammals, so they have to breathe air. When they come up from a dive to breathe at the surface, they are easy to catch and kill in nets, and have now been brought to the brink of extinction. In the past, they could withstand losses from predators such as sharks, killer whales, and estuary crocodiles.

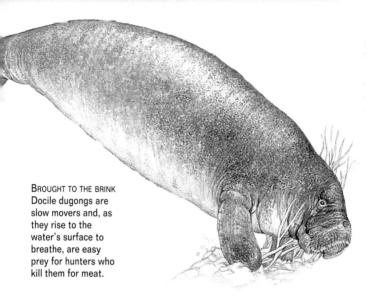

BROUGHT TO THE BRINK
Docile dugongs are slow movers and, as they rise to the water's surface to breathe, are easy prey for hunters who kill them for meat.

Now, with numbers so low, the dugongs could be totally wiped out by such attacks. The plight of the African and Asian populations is cause for extreme concern – although the dugong is protected by law, illegal killing still occurs, sometimes by accident, sometimes deliberately in order to obtain food, hides, and body parts for use in traditional medicines. Dugongs once lived around the Australian coast in their thousands. Even today, groups of several hundred dugongs are still reported off its western coast. In the seas between Australia's northern coast and the island of New Guinea lives the largest dugong population. Here hunting is permitted, though monitored, and over 1,000 animals are killed each year. It remains to be seen if the result will be the eventual extinction of the dugong.

CHIMPANZEE

Pan troglodytes
Family: PONGIDAE
Order: PRIMATES

STATUS: Endangered (IUCN); CITES I. Unknown numbers, but might exceed 150,000. Related endangered species: Western gorilla (*Gorilla gorilla*); orang-utan (*Pongo pygmaeus*); pygmy chimpanzee (*Pan paniscus*).

DISTRIBUTION: Rain forest, deciduous forest, swamp forest, and savanna grassland with access to evergreen fruiting trees in 21 countries in tropical western and central Africa, from Senegal and Angola to Tanzania and Sudan.

SIZE: Length: 28–38in (71–97cm); height at shoulder: 39–66in (95–165cm); males slightly larger than females. Weight: 66–110lb (30–50kg).

FORM: Large ape covered in long, brown-black hair. Palms and face are bare; adults are sometimes bald. Skin on face is wrinkled, usually pink or brown, darkening with age. Projecting jaw has large, expressive lips.

DIET: Fruit, leaves; also seeds, shoots, bark, flowers, honey, and insects; some meat from smaller animals, including monkeys and wild pigs.

BREEDING: Single young born at any time of year after gestation of 7–8 months; weaned at 3–4 years; stays with mother until mature at 7 years. Life span may exceed 60 years!

CONSERVATION: Although wild chimpanzees are protected by law in several African countries, regulations are difficult to enforce, especially in areas of central Africa torn apart by political instability and civil war. In addition, legal protection of the species does not mean protection of their habitat. Tropical forests continue to be logged and cleared for agriculture. In many areas, chimpanzees are treated as pests and killed to protect crops. Some are eaten as bush meat, and body parts are

used in traditional medicines and rituals. Chimpanzees are also captured live and sold as pets or for medical research. There are large numbers of chimpanzees born and bred in captivity, many of them in zoos. Most of these animals are ill-equipped to be returned to the wild. There is more hope for wild-born chimpanzees that have been rescued from illegal collections. These animals can practise their "wild" skills in a rehabilitation center before being released.

CHIMPANZEE COLLAPSE
The number of these primates has shrunk from 2 million to 150,000. Chief threats are the loss of the trees in whose branches they have their sleeping nests. They are also overhunted for food and to protect crops, and are still sold for medical research and as pets.

MOUNTAIN GORILLA

Gorilla beringei beringei
Family: PONGIDAE
Order: PRIMATES

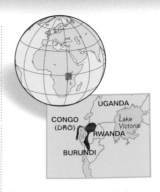

STATUS: Endangered (IUCN);
CITES I. Fewer than 600 remain.
Related endangered species:
Western lowland gorilla *(Gorilla
gorilla gorilla)*; eastern lowland
gorilla (*G. beringei diehli*);
chimpanzee *(Pan troglodytes)*;
pygmy chimpanzee *(P. paniscus)*;
orang-utan *(Pongo pygmaeus)*.

DISTRIBUTION: Remote cloud
forests on volcanic slopes of
mountains linking the Democratic
Republic of Congo, Rwanda, and
Uganda, eastern Africa.

SIZE: Height: Up to 6ft (1.8m);
male up to twice the size of the
female. Weight: 154–440lb
(70–200kg).

FORM: Large, powerful ape. Dark
brown-black hair, longer than that
of lowland gorillas. Walks on all
fours using soles of feet and
knuckles of hands; arms shorter
than those of lowland gorilla.
Dominant males very large with
silvery hair on back.

DIET: Leaves, roots, and shoots;
some bark, flowers, fruit, fungi;
occasionally invertebrates and
even dung.

BREEDING: Single young born at
any time of year after 8–month
gestation; births at intervals of at
least 4 years; young weaned at
3 years; mature at 10 years
(female) or 15 years (male). Life
span up to 30 years in wild.

CONSERVATION: The magnificent
mountain gorilla is especially
vulnerable because of its slow
breeding rate, which makes it
difficult to replenish numbers. Most
females will raise only two to four
young in their 30–year lifetime. The
major threats faced by the
mountain gorilla have been

shooting and habitat loss for timber, fuel, and farmland. Such dangers can be prevented by setting aside areas of gorilla habitat and patrolling them to prevent hunting. Such refuges existed, but the protection provided was often inadequate. Things improved in the 1970s and by the end of the 1980s the gorilla's prospects looked brighter. They became a Rwandan national treasure and the focus of a lucrative ecotourism industry. Then in the 1990s civil war in Rwanda claimed the lives of half a million people and left 750,000 homeless. Refugees seeking water and bushmeat entered the parks and trapped many gorillas. International conservation efforts are trying to redress the balance.

VICTIMS OF CIVIL WARS
Half of all known mountain gorillas live in the Virunga volcanoes region and the rest are in the Bwindi Impenetrable National Park in eastern Africa. Escaping refugees spilled into these areas and killed these primates for bushmeat.

ORANG-UTAN

Pongo pygmaeus
Family: PONGIDAE
Order: PRIMATES

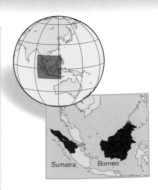

Sumatra   Borneo

STATUS: Endangered (IUCN); CITES I. Fewer than 30,000 remain. Related endangered species: Western lowland gorilla *(Gorilla gorilla gorilla)*; mountain gorilla *(G. beringei beringei)*; pygmy chimpanzee *(Pan paniscus)*; chimpanzee *(P. troglodytes)*.

DISTRIBUTION: Rain forests in Indonesia (Kalimantan, Sumatra) and Malaysia (Sabah, Sarawak).

SIZE: Height: male 54in (137cm); female 45in (115cm). Weight: male 130–200lb (60–90kg); female 88–110lb (40–50kg).

FORM: A large, long-haired ape; coat is usually reddish, but varies from orange to dark chocolate.

DIET: Mainly fruit; also young leaves and shoots, insects, bark, and small mammals.

BREEDING: Usually gives birth to single young; mature at 7–10 years. Life span up to 40 years.

CONSERVATION: Once orang-utans were found throughout Southeast Asia and southern China, but during the 1990s, the numbers declined by up to 50 percent. The greatest threat to orang-utans is the destruction of their tropical rain forest habitat. Large areas of forest have been affected as trees are felled for timber, and land cleared for farming. Another threat is the capture of live orangs for the pet trade. For every animal that survives capture and shipment, five or six others will die in the process. This highly intelligent species is protected by law in Indonesia and Malaysia, both countries having signed up to CITES. The 1987 Asia Primate Action Plan identified conservation measures needed.

They included
setting up and
managing protected
areas, surveys to
establish the orang-utan
population, and a public
education program. About 60
percent of orang-utans in Borneo
could be protected if conservation
laws were enforced. A number of
orang-utan rehabilitation centers
look after orang-utans rescued
from smugglers or those whose
forest homes have been logged.
The apes are then relocated to
protected areas.

STILL THREATENED
Orang-utans once
numbered hundreds of
thousands but numbers
have declined sharply
because of loss of
habitat and capture for
the pet trade.

BLACK GIBBON

Hylobates concolor
Family: HYLOBATIDAE
Order: PRIMATES

STATUS: Endangered (IUCN); CITES I. About 5,000 are thought to be in China; populations elsewhere much smaller and all declining. Related endangered species: Silvery gibbon (*Hylobates moloch*).

DISTRIBUTION: Closed canopy evergreen forests in Cambodia, Vietnam, Laos, and south China.

SIZE: Height: 18–25in (46–48cm). Weight: 11–17lb (5–8kg).

FORM: Slender ape with long arms and hook-shaped hands; fur dense and silky. Mature males black with white cheeks; breeding females pale buff.

DIET: Ripe fruit, tender young leaves, and buds; invertebrates.

BREEDING: 1 young born every 2–3 years; gestation of 7–8 months; weaned at about 2 years.

CONSERVATION: The playfully acrobatic antics of black gibbon babies swinging through the high forest canopy has resulted in many of them being taken from the wild to be kept as pets. Without their mothers, they cannot learn essential skills and end up lonely and depressed in captivity. In China black gibbons are legally protected, and many live in reserves.

Nevertheless, people break the law to obtain black gibbon meat, and bones for use in eastern medicines. In addition, local human populations have increased by about 50 percent in 25 years, resulting in a disastrous drop in gibbon numbers. Allowing them to become extinct would have dire consequences for the ecosystem as the gibbons, being fruit eaters, help disperse forest tree seeds in their dung. On a note of optimism, it seems that gibbons can return to areas of previously felled trees that have regenerated. With careful management it should be possible to restore black gibbon populations to some of their habitats.

FOREST FRIENDLY
Black gibbons are distinctive and social creatures that bring benefits to their forest habitats through their dispersing of fruit seeds. If they survive they can live up to 25 years in the wild.

DRILL

Mandrillus leucophaeus
Family: CERCOPITHECIDAE
Order: PRIMATES

STATUS: Endangered (IUCN); CITES I. 3,000 or fewer survive. Related endangered species; Various macaques, monkeys, and apes, including the mandrill (*Mandrillus sphinx*).

DISTRIBUTION: Lowland forest in Cameroon, southeastern Nigeria, and Bioko Island (Equatorial Guinea).

SIZE: Length: 18–35.5in (45–90cm); male up to twice as big as female. Weight: about 33lb (15kg).

FORM: Large, stout-bodied baboon with short tail. Large head with black face fringed with white fur; fur elsewhere grayish brown. Males have mane of thicker fur and hairless buttocks of varying shades of red, pink, and blue.

DIET: Fruit, seeds, roots, fungi, insects, and some small vertebrates.

Mandrill, a related endangered species

BREEDING: Single young born at any time of year, but mostly December–April after gestation period of about 8 months, mature at 5 years. Life span up to 29 years.

CONSERVATION: The drill – a powerful, stocky type of baboon – has a range of only about 15,000 square miles (40,000 sq. km), with most of the remaining population living in one national park in Cameroon. The drills are omnivores that prefer to live in mature, untouched forest, known as primary forest, but they have begun to return to areas where felled trees have been allowed to regenerate. However, very few areas have been allowed to return to nature in this way. Most trees are planted with crops, which the drills eat, and they are then killed as pests. They are also hunted for their meat. To secure a safe future for the drill, a protected and suitable habitat needs to be set aside. A conservation plan must include educating local people of the need to stop hunting the drills.

EMERGENCY EFFORTS
The drill (right) is a little smaller than its relative the mandrill (left) and has an all-black face with white hair. Emergency measures are needed to prevent this vulnerable species from disappearing along with its lowland forest habitat.

HAIRY-EARED DWARF LEMUR

Allocebus trichotis
Family: CHEIROGALEIDAE
Order: PRIMATES

MADAGASCAR

STATUS: Endangered (IUCN); CITES I. Fewer than 1,000 remain. Related endangered species: Coquerel's mouse lemur (*Mirza coquereli*).

DISTRIBUTION: Lowland rain forests in Mananara, eastern Madagascar.

SIZE: Length head/body: 5–6in (12.5–15.2cm); tail 6–7.5in (14.9–19.5cm). Weight: 2.6–3.4oz (75–98g).

FORM: Minute, dormouselike lemur with fuzzy, brownish-gray fur and a long, furry tail; eyes are large and black; ears are adorned with tufts of long fur; large hands and feet.

DIET: Large insects including crickets; fruit, and other plant material; honey.

BREEDING: Single young born in January or February after 8–week gestation. Life span unknown.

CONSERVATION: Looking more like a mouse than a monkey, the hairy-eared dwarf lemur is one of the world's smallest and most endangered primates. It is shy, nocturnal, and hardly ever comes down from the trees. More than once the hairy-eared dwarf lemur has been believed to be extinct. Between 1875 and 1966 there were no reports of any sightings. Then in 1991 four individuals were caught during a scientific expedition and kept in captivity. Most of what has been discovered about the species' biology came from studying these specimens. All lemurs are protected by law in Madagascar, but controls are difficult to enforce, and illegal trapping continues to put the hairy-eared dwarf lemur at risk.

A greater threat to the animal is the destruction of the lowland forest, and the species' future now lies in its survival in regenerated woodlands or in the scraps of forest that are left. It is proposed that a large area of rain forest should be protected to conserve the species. Captive breeding and releases back into the wild may also help boost numbers and increase scientific understanding of the species.

SINGLE-ISLAND PRIMATE
The hairy-eared dwarf lemur is a rare primate that has only ever been found in a small area of eastern Madagascar. A concerted effort is urgently needed to safeguard its habitat and ensure the animal's survival.

LONG-BEAKED ECHIDNA

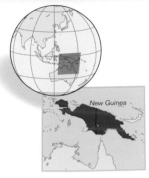

Zaglossus bruijni
Family: TACHYGLOSSIDAE
Order: MONOTREMATA

STATUS: Endangered (IUCN); CITES I. Population unknown, but probably low thousands. Related endangered species: Short-beaked echidna (*Tachyglossus aculeatus multiaculeatus*).

DISTRIBUTION: Various habitats from lowland tropical jungles to mountain forests and grasslands at more than 13,000ft (4,000m) above sea level on the island of New Guinea (containing Papua New Guinea and West Irian, a province of Indonesia).

SIZE: Length: 18–30in (45–77cm); height at shoulder: about 10in (25cm). Weight: 11–22lb (5–10kg).

FORM: A small animal covered in short, thick spines and dense, black hair. Long, tubular, downcurved snout. Weak jaw with no teeth. Feet have large claws; hind ones point sideways; walks slowly with rolling gait.

DIET: Mainly earthworms.

FOREST FELLING
They are hunted for food and suffer from destruction of their forest home. Protection in the nature reserves of New Guinea is their main hope.

BREEDING: Probably lays 1 egg per year in July; egg is incubated in temporary pouch on the mother's belly. Young fed on milk for several months before independence.
A long-beaked echidna has lived more than 30 years in captivity; life span in the wild unknown.

CONSERVATION: The long-beaked echidna pokes its snout into wet forest leaf litter in search of worms and grubs. When the forests are cut down, the ground dries out, and the animal's diet becomes less abundant. Felling trees also removes the availability of rotting wood, a vital source of invertebrate food. Large areas of forest have been cleared in New Guinea and the echidnas can now only survive in remote areas. They are no longer found in most of the northern areas of the island. Long-beaked echidnas are not at risk from natural predators, so their spines have evolved to offer only limited protection against hunting dogs, used to trap them for their highly-prized meat. The echidna breeds very slowly, and so is unable to sustain heavy losses. Few are kept in captivity, so there is little prospect of developing a "safety net" of captive-bred echidnas as an insurance against their extinction.

KANGAROO ISLAND DUNNART

Sminthopsis aitkeni
Family: DASYURIDAE
Order: DASYUROMORPHIA

AUSTRALIA

STATUS: Endangered (IUCN); not listed by CITES. Population unknown, but tiny. Related endangered species: Boullanger Island gray-bellied dunnart (*Sminthopsis grisoventer*); Julia Creejk dunnart (*S. douglasi*); sandhill dunnart (*S. psammophilla*); Butler's dunnart (*S. butleri*); Queensland common dunnart (*S. murina tatei*).

DISTRIBUTION: Mallee (scrub) heathland on Kangaroo Island, South Australia.

SIZE: Length head/body: 3–4in (7.6–10cm); tail: 3.5–4in (9–10cm); male about 10% larger than female. Weight: 0.7–0.9oz (20–25g).

FORM: Mouselike marsupial with long, tapering snout and long tail; fur grayish tinged with sooty black on back.

DIET: Probably insectivorous, like its close relative the common dunnart.

BREEDING: Probably similar to common dunnart, with large litters born after short gestation; young weaned at about 2 months.

CONSERVATION: Until the late 1960s there were thought to be no dunnarts living on Kangaroo Island off the coast of South Australia. Then in 1969 a domestic dog captured and killed two specimens of what appeared to be the common dunnart. By the mid-1980s science had progressed sufficiently for the creatures to be identified as a separate species. The newly named Kangaroo Island dunnart was a conservation worry because no populations existed elsewhere. Little is known about the animal. The lack of sightings can be partly explained by the fact

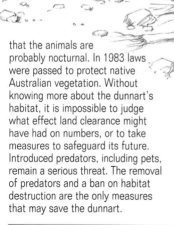

that the animals are probably nocturnal. In 1983 laws were passed to protect native Australian vegetation. Without knowing more about the dunnart's habitat, it is impossible to judge what effect land clearance might have had on numbers, or to take measures to safeguard its future. Introduced predators, including pets, remain a serious threat. The removal of predators and a ban on habitat destruction are the only measures that may save the dunnart.

RARE SIGHTINGS
The Kangaroo Island dunnart has only been spotted a handful of times. Efforts are underway to find out more about this rare and elusive endangered island mammal so that it can be conserved.

MAHOGANY GLIDER

Petaurus gracilis
Family: PETAURIDAE
Order: DIPROTODONTIA

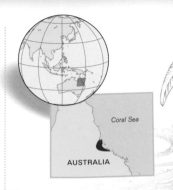

Coral Sea

AUSTRALIA

STATUS: Endangered (IUCN); not listed by CITES. Population estimated at 2,000–3,000 in 1989, but probably fewer remain. Related endangered species: Leadbeater's possum (*Gymnobelideus leadbeateri*); Tate's triok (*Dactilopsila tatei*).

DISTRIBUTION: Coastal tropical forest, no higher than 400ft (120m) above sea level on Northern Queensland coast, Australia.

SIZE: Length head/body: 8–10.5in (21.5–26.5cm); tail: 12–15in (30–38cm); male about 10 percent bigger than female. Weight: 9–15oz (250–400g).

FORM: Gray, cat-sized marsupial with long, furry tail. Flaps of skin between front and back legs become sails when limbs are extended in gliding.

DIET: Nectar, sap, and gum of coastal forest trees; some invertebrates and lichens.

BREEDING: Litters of 1 or 2 young; little else is known about its breeding biology.

CONSERVATION: The graceful mahogany glider was first discovered in 1883, but it wasn't until 1989 that a living population was found. However, within a month of the animal's rediscovery the glider's forest habitat had been felled and replanted. Fortunately, in the following years further populations of mahogany glider were found nearby, but with each new discovery came the growing realization that the species was in real trouble. More than 80 percent of its coastal habitat had already been destroyed and the remaining forest was in danger of being cleared.

The mahogany glider was declared an endangered species in 1994 and as much glider habitat as possible was purchased. Landowners who did not want to sell the land were asked instead to guarantee the security of their forests in order to conserve the gliders. After more than a decade of intensive study we know a lot more about the mahogany glider. More research into its habits will ensure the best protection for this creature.

ONLY IN QUEENSLAND
The mahogany glider has a long tail to form a counter-balance when scrambling around in trees. This marsupial mammal is now restricted to a small strip of coast in northern Queensland.

MARSUPIAL MOLE

Notoryctes typhlops
Family: NOTORYCTIDAE
Order: NOTORYCTEMORPHIA

AUSTRALIA

STATUS: Endangered (IUCN); not listed by CITES. Almost impossible to estimate population. Related endangered species: Northern marsupial mole *(Notoryctes caurinus)*; although it may not qualify as a separate species. Its scientific classification is the subject of a debate.

DISTRIBUTION: Desert burrows in northwestern Australia.

SIZE: Length head/body: 4–6in (10–16cm); tail: 1in (2.4cm). Weight: 1.2–2.5oz (35–70g).

FORM: Flat-bodied animal with pale-golden fur; very short legs; spadelike front feet; no functional eyes; ear hole hidden in fur; nose has tough, horny shield; tail short and stubby. Female has a pouch opening to rear.

DIET: Insect grubs, particularly larvae of beetles and moths.

BREEDING: Unknown.

CONSERVATION: Since they normally spend their entire lives buried in the sandy soil of Australia's western deserts, little is known about the elusive marsupial moles. Before declaring an animal Endangered, the IUCN normally needs convincing scientific evidence that the species is likely to become extinct unless the causes of the declining numbers are removed. In the case of the marsupial moles the IUCN agreed to classify the species as Endangered (even though most scientists who have tried to study the species admit that they have no idea how many marsupial moles there may be). So few have ever been caught that it has proved almost impossible to find out anything about their lifestyle.

Until researchers can get some idea of population size it will remain very difficult to prove what its current status is. Marsupial moles have been killed out of curiosity or for their silky fur, but are not deliberately hunted. Their chief problem is likely to be changes in habitat due to burning of grassland for grazing pasture. Introduced species, such as cats, could be a problem too, in addition to natural predators, such as foxes.

DIFFICULT TO MONITOR
So few marsupial moles have been monitored because they rarely surface above ground. When they do it is usually after rain, and their bodies leave distinctive furrows in the sand. The mole has no eyes or obvious ears, which would clog with sand.

PROSPERINE ROCK WALLABY

Petrogale persephone
Family: MACROPODIDAE
Order: DIPROTODONTIA

STATUS: Endangered (IUCN); not listed by CITES. Unknown population. At least 16 other species of wallaby and kangaroo, including Goodfellow's tree kangaroo *(Dendrolagus goodfellow) are* related endangered species.

DISTRIBUTION: Deciduous coastal forests with grassy areas and rocky outcrops in northeastern Queensland and Whitsunday Bay, Australia.

SIZE: Length head/body: 19.5in (50–64cm); tail: 20–27in (51–68cm); male up to 50% larger than female. Weight: 9–20lb (4 9kg).

FORM: Dog-sized animal with dark-gray fur tinged with red in places especially around ears, face, and shoulders; white fur on chin blends with pale underside; feet and tail strikingly black.

DIET: Grasses.

BREEDING: Single young born any time of year; no further details.

CONSERVATION: Today's population of Prosperine rock wallabies appears to be all that remains of a once widespread animal. Gradual changes in climate and vegetation over the last two million years have not suited the species. It has been edged out of most of its former range by two better-adapted forms of rock wallaby. The remaining population lives in a part of the Queensland coast that is increasingly popular with tourists and its habitat is being developed. However, there are smaller populations of the wallabies on several nearby islands, some of which are national parks and free from developers and predators, such as dingoes and large dogs. In the future, the wallaby populations could be boosted by reintroducing captive-bred individuals.

IN THE BALANCE
A recent addition to the Australian list of scientifically described mammal species, this wallaby is in danger of disappearing before it has been fully studied.

ESKIMO CURLEW

Numenius borealis
Family: SCOLOPACIDAE
Order: CHARADRIIFORMES

STATUS: Critically Endangered: (IUCN); CITES I. If it still survives, the population is tiny. Related endangered species: Bristle-thighed curlew (Numenius tahitiensis); Far Eastern curlew (N. madagascariensis); long-billed curlew (N. americanus); slender-billed curlew (N. tenuirostris).

DISTRIBUTION: Winters in wet grasslands, intertidal habitats, and semidesert and breeds at 2 locations in Northwest Territories, Canada. Migrates to northeastern Argentina via tallgrass and mixed-grass prairies of North America. Return migration thought to be up Pacific coast of South America; lands on Texas coast before drifting northward to the breeding sites.

SIZE: Length: 11.5–13.5in (29–34cm); wingspan: 32–33.5in (81–85cm). Weight: 9.5–16oz (270–454g).

FORM: Small, cinnamon-colored bird with downcurved bill.

Wings extend beyond tip of tail; cinnamon below; heavily barred breast and Y-shaped flank marks.

DIET: In Northwest territories: ants, grubs, freshwater insects, and crowberries. During migration: on rocky coastlines snails, worms, and other invertebrates; in uplands mainly crowberries; south of crowberry range and in Argentina, insects. On return migration in North American prairies, diet included the now extinct Rocky Mountain grasshopper.

BREEDING: Four eggs laid May–August.

CONSERVATION: The Eskimo curlew probably once had a population of hundreds of thousands, but it declined suddenly in the 19th century. The last confirmed sighting in 1985, with a number of unconfirmed sightings since then. The decline was due to the hunting of large numbers along spring migratory paths in North America. Another factor is the near total loss of the North American tallgrass prairie ecosystem to farming. This conversion of the birds' habitat was combined with the suppression of prairie wildfires and led to a reduction in the number of recently burned areas preferred by the Eskimo curlew. In addition, the Rocky Mountain grasshopper – a key food source – became extinct. If the Eskimo curlew isn't already extinct, it has left an important message about the need to manage prairie habitats for wildlife as well as food production, if other species are not to go the same way.

IS IT EXTINCT?
The Eskimo curlew once existed in large numbers. It may now be extinct as a result of hunting and habitat destruction. Since the mid-1980s there have been only unconfirmed reports of its existence.

JAPANESE MURRELET

*Synthliboramphus
wumizusume*
Family: ALCIDAE
Order: CHARADRIIFORMES

JAPAN

STATUS: Vulnerable (IUCN); not listed by CITES. Population of 5,000–6,000, possibly 10,000 birds. Related endangered species: Craven's murrelet (*Synthliboramphus craveri*); Xantus's murrelet *(S. hypoleucus)*; marbled murrelet (*Brachyramphus marmoratus*).

DISTRIBUTION: Feeds in warm ocean currents off coasts and islands around Japan; breeds on small, uninhabited islands around central and southern Japan; possibly breeds in Russia, too.

SIZE: Length: 10in (25cm). Weight: 6oz (170g).

FORM: A small, squat auk with a short neck, short wings, and short tail. Black head with (in summer only) black crest and white stripes extending from eyes to nape; black and blue-gray upperparts; dark-gray flanks; white underparts; short, thick, blue-gray bill; grayish-yellow legs and feet.

DIET: Krill and other planktonic crustaceans, plus shrimp and small larval fish such as herring, smelt, and sandeels.

BREEDING: Pairs for life, nesting from mid-February to early May in pairs or small colonies, using rock crevices, hollows, and burrows. Two eggs are incubated for about 4.5–5 weeks by both parents. Chicks leave nest within 2 days of hatching and follow parents to sea, to be reared until fully grown at about 1 month old.

CONSERVATION: This stout little murrelet breeds only on a scattering of rocky islands off the coasts of central and southern Japan.

Here there were once no land predators. Now black rats, probably accidentally introduced by fishermen, feast on the unattended eggs. Recently the birds have had to compete with humans for the small crustaceans and fish on which the murrelets feed. They are frequently trapped in deadly drift nets, while others are poisoned by oil dumped at sea. Saving the murrelet will involve getting rid of land predators and restricting human access.

TRAPPED IN NETS
The Japanese murrelet may still be able to hold its own if its breeding colonies are made secure. New reserves are planned, but ways to reduce the number of birds trapped in fishing nets need working on, too.

JERDON'S COURSER

Rhinoptilus bitorquatus
Family: GLAREOLIDAE
Order: CHARADRIIFORMES

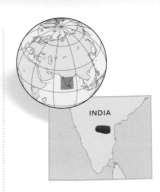

INDIA

STATUS: Critically Endangered: (IUCN); not listed by CITES. It is estimated that 50–250 exist. Related endangered species: Black-winged pratincole *(Glareola nordmanni)*.

DISTRIBUTION: Rolling, rocky foothills with dense scrub forest and bushes (including thorny and nonthorny species), interspersed with open areas of bare ground in Eastern Ghats (mountain range) of states of Andhra Pradesh, and extreme southern Madhya Pradesh in eastern India.

SIZE: Length: about 10.5in (27cm).

FORM: Slender-bodied, smallish, ploverlike bird; shortish, yellow-based, black arched bill; longish, pale-yellowish legs. Plumage has complex pattern with distinctive pair of brown breast bands (the upper one much broader) separated by a white band; mainly blackish-brown crown and hind neck; broad, white eyestripes and broad, blackish-brown band behind each eye; orange-chestnut patch on white throat; upperparts mainly brown, apart from pattern of breast banding; underparts mainly white; black tail with white base.

DIET: Poorly known; feeds at night, probably on insects.

BREEDING: Unconfirmed report of clutch of 2 eggs said to have been collected in 1895.

CONSERVATION: This enigmatic and delicately built wader made ornithological history when it was rediscovered in eastern India after being thought extinct since the early 20th century. Today there probably exists a single, small population in three hill ranges.

The Jerdon's courser is under great threat since 57 villages were relocated from a region due to be flooded to within the birds' range. A further threat comes from quarrying operations. In an effort to save the little-known bird from extinction, a wildlife sanctuary and national park have been set up. More needs to be known about the courser, including its distribution and feeding habits, in order to help protect it.

REDISCOVERED WADER
The Jerdon's courser with its distinctive double breast-band was thought to be extinct until recently rediscovered in eastern India.

BERMUDA PETREL

Pterodroma cahow
Family: PROCELLARIIDAE
Order: PROCELLARIIFORMES

USA

Bermuda

STATUS: Endangered (IUCN); not listed by CITES. Fewer than 200 birds exist. Related to several other endangered petrels including Chatham Islands petrel (*Pterodroma axillaris*), Atlantic petrel (*P. incerta*) and Murphy's petrel (*P. ultima*).

DISTRIBUTION: Breeds on rocky islets in Castle Harbor, Bermuda; outside the breeding season (mid-June–October) lives at sea, probably wandering across the Atlantic Ocean; has been recorded off North Carolina.

SIZE: Length: 15in (38cm); wingspan: 35in (89cm).

FORM: Medium-sized, long-winged, short-tailed seabird with hooked black bill bearing nostrils in tubes on top; webbed feet set at hind end of body.

DIET: Little known; probably mainly squid and crustaceans, plus some fish.

BREEDING: January to mid-June; colonies once nested in burrows in soil, but now use natural crevices in soft limestone and artificial burrows; single, large white egg is incubated for 7–8 weeks; young fledge in 13–14 weeks.

CONSERVATION: Also known as the cahow in imitation of its eerie mating calls, the Bermuda petrel is a graceful, long-winged bird, fast in flight. The 150 or so islands of Bermuda are home to this rare seabird. The islands remained uninhabited until 1609, when an English expedition was shipwrecked there. The settlers brought pigs and rats that raided the petrels' nesting burrows.

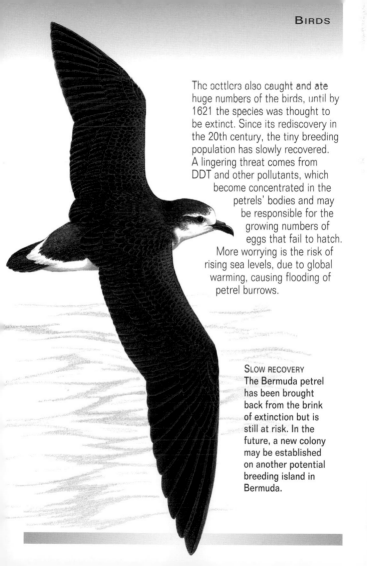

The settlers also caught and ate huge numbers of the birds, until by 1621 the species was thought to be extinct. Since its rediscovery in the 20th century, the tiny breeding population has slowly recovered. A lingering threat comes from DDT and other pollutants, which become concentrated in the petrels' bodies and may be responsible for the growing numbers of eggs that fail to hatch. More worrying is the risk of rising sea levels, due to global warming, causing flooding of petrel burrows.

SLOW RECOVERY
The Bermuda petrel has been brought back from the brink of extinction but is still at risk. In the future, a new colony may be established on another potential breeding island in Bermuda.

WANDERING ALBATROSS

Diomedea exulans
Family: DIOMEDEIDAE
Order: PROCELLARIIFORMES

STATUS: Vulnerable (IUCN); not listed by CITES. Some 28,000 mature adults, 8,500 breeding pairs exist. Related endangered species include Tristan albatross *(Diomedea dabbenena),* and Antipodean albatross *(D. antipodensis).*

DISTRIBUTION: Windswept skies over the Southern Ocean, breeding on exposed ridges and slopes among patchy vegetation on islands of South Georgia, Prince Edward Island, Marion Island, the Crozet Islands, Kerguélen Islands, and Macquarie Island.

SIZE: Length: 3.5–4.4ft (1–1.3m); wingspan: 8.3–11.5ft (2.5–3.5m). Weight: 14–25lb (6.2–11.3kg).

FORM: Huge, sleek ocean bird with long, hooked bill, tubular nostrils, webbed feet, and very long, slender wings adapted for soaring and gliding over the ocean. Mainly white with dark upper wings that become whiter with age from the center outward.

DIET: Mainly squid; also carrion and scraps dumped from ships.

BREEDING: Breeds once every 2 years in loose colonies, laying single white, red-flecked egg in a ground nest of mud and grass. Egg incubated by both parents taking shifts of 2–3 weeks for 10–11 weeks; chick fledges in over 9 months.

CONSERVATION: For centuries, the majestic wandering albatross followed ships to scavenge edible scraps thrown overboard. When drift nets were banned in 1993, fishing fleets introduced a technique called longlining.

The boats trailed immensely long lines, with many branch lines attached, each with a hook baited with fish or squid – the albatross's main prey. The birds tried to snatch the bait and were hooked themselves. Thousands of albatrosses died this way each year. This situation can be avoided

in a number of ways. The boats can trail bird-scaring streamers to keep the birds away. They can also add weights to the lines so they sink more quickly, and they can avoid using frozen bait that floats. They can also fish at night, when the birds are less active. They can even use a system that streams the baited lines down tubes so that they emerge underwater, out of sight of the birds. As a result, fleets have reduced seabird catches by 90 percent. Unfortunately illegal "pirate" longlining still kills 10,000 to 20,000 albatrosses each year.

SNAGGED IN LINES
The wandering albatross lives far from human habitation, riding the winds above the stormy Southern Ocean. Yet despite its remote habitat, it faces a threat from industrial fishing fleets that could eliminate the species: the birds get caught in the long floating lines as they seek squid or fish.

LABRADOR DUCK

*Camptorhynchus
labradorius*
Family: ANATIDAE
Order: ANSERIFORMES

STATUS: Extinct (IUCN); not listed by CITES. Related endangered species: Chubut steamerduck (*Tachyeres leucocephalus*).

DISTRIBUTION: Unknown; probably bred along the Gulf of St. Lawrence and coastal Labrador, Canada, and wintered along seacoasts from Nova Scotia to Chesapeake Bay, Virginia.

SIZE: Length head/body: 12–15in (30–40cm); tail: 2in (5cm).

FORM: Male strikingly black and white; female brown.

DIET: Unknown; probably a specialized diet, perhaps soft plant material or invertebrates such as mollusks.

BREEDING: Unknown.

CONSERVATION: Unfortunately, there is very little information available about the distinctive and attractive Labrador duck.

Despite the fact that they were seen regularly in meat markets on the east coast of the USA, they were not a popular food, and it would appear that nobody made a special effort to hunt them. This is in direct contrast to many extinct and endangered bird species that were sought after and hunted down ruthlessly. Instead, the Labrador duck seems never to have been a successful or abundant species and appears to have died out from natural causes. It disappeared from American markets between 1850 and 1870. The last recorded specimen was probably one shot in the fall of 1875 on Long Island, New York. The Labrador duck is one of five or six species of American birds that have become extinct in the last 200 years.

DISAPPEARING DUCK
This duck was never very common and its habits and lifestyle are still unknown. It became extinct in the late 19th century, but the reason for its disappearance remains a mystery.

NENE

Branta sandvicensis
Family: ANATIDAE
Order: ANSERIFORMES

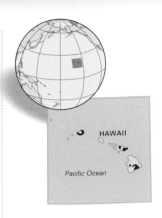

Pacific Ocean

HAWAII

STATUS: Vulnerable (IUCN); CITES I. Probably fewer than 1,000 remain. Related endangered species include Laysan duck (*Anas laysanensis*) and Hawaiian duck (*A. wyvilliana*).

DISTRIBUTION: Originally throughout Hawaiian archipelago, but reduced to a few wild birds on Hawaii by 1950. Following reintroductions, it now lives wild on grassy shrublands and sparsely vegetated, semiarid basalt lava flows on volcanic slopes on Hawaii and Maui, and on lowland pasture on Kauai.

SIZE: Length: 25–27in (63–69cm). Weight: 2.9–6.6lb (1.3–3kg).

FORM: Small, erect goose with short wings, long legs, and strong feet with reduced webbing. Black bill, face, and crown; golden-buff neck with unique dark furrows; upperparts and breast sepia brown with pattern of dark gray and white; white belly.

DIET: Moist vegetation such as grass, leaves, berries; also seeds.

BREEDING: Birds pair for life and breed in November–January; 3–5 white eggs laid in a nest scrape and incubated by female for about 4 weeks while male stands guard; young fledge in about 10–12 weeks.

CONSERVATION: Unique to the Hawaiian Islands, the nene was brought almost to the point of extinction, first by the Polynesians, who arrived on the islands about 1,600 years ago. They introduced pigs, dogs, and rats, all of which played havoc with the ground-nesting nene.

From the 18th century, European settlers brought more killers: black rats, cats, and the Indian mongoose. By 1949 there were perhaps only 30 left. The recovery of the nene is mostly due to captive breeding programs. Conservation bodies now aim to create large, predator-free reserves in lowland areas. The elimination of poaching and reduction of roadkill are also planned.

CAPTIVE BREEDING SUCCESS
The nene was driven to the verge of extinction by the destruction of its wild habitats and the introduction of predators. It may soon be thriving again thanks to captive breeding.

ATITLÁN GREBE

Podilymbus gigas
Family: PODICIPEDIDAE
Order: PODICIPEDIFORMES

GUATEMALA

STATUS: Extinct: (IUCN); CITES I. Related endangered species include Alaotra grebe *(Tachybaptus rufolavatus)*, Junin grebe *(Podiceps taczanowskii)*, hooded grebe *(P. gallardoi)*, and Colombian grebe *(P. andinus)*.

DISTRIBUTION: Shoreline of Lake Atitlán, Guatemala.

SIZE: Length: 13–16in (33–40.5cm).

FORM: Big-headed, thick-necked, dumpy-bodied, tailless waterbird; stout whitish or pale-grayish bill with black vertical band; upperparts dark brownish; darker on head and neck; narrow whitish ring around eye; underparts dull creamy-buff. Juveniles had pale neck stripes.

DIET: 50 percent was *Potamocarcinus* crabs that thrived among aquatic vegetation along edge of lake; also small fish and insects and snails. (Large-mouthed bass competed with grebe for food.)

BREEDING: From March with egg-laying peak in April; sometimes nested all year round. Solitary breeders; nest a floating platform of aquatic vegetation anchored to submerged plants; 1–5 whitish eggs stained by vegetation. Chicks independent at 10–12 weeks.

CONSERVATION: There may never have been more than about 400 Atitlán Grebes. In 1958, and again in 1960, the large-mouthed sea bass was introduced to Gautemala's Lake Atitlán to attract tourist anglers. The fish thrived by eating the grebe's food, and preying on its young, too. By 1965 there were only 80 birds surviving. A conservation project was begun and by 1975 the birds were back to 232 in number.

However, recovery was short lived. Land around the shore was sold for building, while the reed beds in which the grebe nested were also cut down – by 1980, 60 percent of the reeds had disappeared. An earthquake in 1976 saw the water level fall drastically and in 1983 the warden recruited to protect the birds was shot by guerrillas. A 1987 survey of the lake, which has a shoreline of 78 miles (125 km), failed to find any Atitlán grebes and it was declared extinct.

DECLARED EXTINCT
The Atitlán grebe was a flightless bird that coexisted with people for centuries, until introduced fish, increased development and tourism, and natural disasters conspired to destroy its habitat.

ALGERIAN NUTHATCH

Sitta ledanti
Family: SITTIDAE
Order: PASSERIFORMES

ALGERIA

STATUS: Endangered (IUCN); not listed by CITES. About 1,000–2,500 birds remain. Related endangered species: giant nuthatch (*Sitta magna*); White-browed nuthatch (*S. victoriae*); beautiful nuthatch (*S. formosa*).

DISTRIBUTION: Restricted to one small area: the oak forest on mountain summits at about 6,500ft (2,000m) in northeastern Algeria; also regenerated oak forest from 2,900–4,600ft (900–1,400m) in same region.

SIZE: Length: 5in (13cm). Weight: 0.6oz (16–18g).

FORM: Small, dumpy bird with a relatively large head. Slender, mainly black bill with wedge-shaped tip; short tail. Upperparts blue-gray with bold whitish stripe above each eye; blackish stripe on cap, forecrown, and through eye in males and to a lesser extent in females; underparts creamy-pink to orange-buff; gray legs and feet.

DIET: In summer mainly insects and spiders with some seeds; in winter mainly seeds and nuts of trees.

BREEDING: May to June. Nest of woodchips, leaves, feathers, and hog bristles prepared in a tree hole 10–50ft (3–15m) above ground, usually in dead fir or cedar, but also in oaks. Common brood size is 2, with a maximum of 4; incubation period not recorded; fledgling time probably 3–3.5 weeks.

CONSERVATION: Known to science only since 1975, the tree-dwelling Algerian nuthatch lives only in the Petite Kabylie Mountains in northern Algeria. Although one of

UNKNOWN FOR SO LONG
The Algerian nuthatch was not known about until 1975. It was discovered by a Belgian botanist, Jean-Pierre Ledant and two companions when climbing the 6,454-ft (1,995-m) peak Djebel Babor. The bird's limited distribution in the mountain forests of northern Algeria helped account for its elusiveness.

its habitats, the Djebel Babor peak, lies within a national park, the nuthatch population there is not entirely secure. Fires have reduced the area of original native forest on the mountain slopes, which are now dominated by cedars. Large numbers of livestock graze the hillsides, preventing trees from regenerating. Woodcutting also removes some of the birds' potential nesting sites. A track was laid up the mountain in the 1970s and the resulting traffic has caused erosion in the area. Disturbance from tourists and increased risk of fires adds to the list of threats. However, the nuthatch is a protected species in Algeria, and the largest surviving population –in the Taza National Park –is not considered at risk from habitat loss.

Archbold's Bowerbird

Archboldia papuensis
Family: Ptilonorhynchidae
Order: Passeriformes

Status: Lower Risk (IUCN); not listed by CITES. Population unknown. Related endangered species: Firemaned bowerbird (*Seiculus bakeri*).

Distribution: Mossy mountain forest of southern beech, Pandanus palm, tree ferns, and dense stands of bamboo in central New Guinea, mainly above 6,500ft (2,000m). The bird is patchily distributed in the remote and little accessed higher mountain forests in the central ranges of the island, and in the east, where they are found in a small range of just 300 square miles (800sq km).

Size: Length: 14.5in (37cm).

Form: The Archbold's bowerbird is a large, jaylike bird with a short, stout bill. Male is black with a bright-yellow crest extending from forehead to neck; female is dull black with ocher markings on her wing primaries; the juvenile male is gray with no yellow crest.

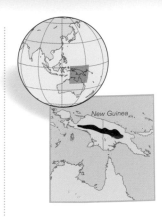

New Guinea

Diet: Mainly fruit; also buds, flowers, seeds, succulent stems, and leaves; a few small animals.

Breeding: The male is somewhat promiscuous, attracting females to mate by displaying and calling from his bower, or display mat. The female builds a nest in a tree. The female incubates the eggs and rears the young alone in the tree.

CONSERVATION: Archbold's bowerbird is one of the spectacular birds of paradise that are famous for their breathtaking courtship displays. In the eastern part of the island, the birds are threatened by logging in two of their forest strongholds, and as their habitats contract, the birds may soon be in trouble. Elsewhere, local populations seem to be larger, and their habitats are still intact, but this may change, and conservationists are concerned for the bird's future. Formerly classified as Vulnerable, it is now considered to be less at risk but is still listed as Near Threatened. Its IUCN classification is a clear warning that if habitat destruction from logging continues at the present rate, the bird may soon join the danger list.

LOGGING INTRUSION
A male Archbold's bowerbird attracts female mates by his prowess at building and decorating a bower. The bird's long-term survival is now in question, due to the steady destruction of its native forests.

BLACK-CAPPED MANAKIN

Piprites pileatus
Family: PIPRIDAE
Order: PASSERIFORMES

BRAZIL

STATUS: Vulnerable (IUCN); not listed by CITES. The population is estimated to be fewer than 10.000 birds. Related endangered species: Araripe manakin (*Antilophia bokermanni*); Wied's tyrant-manakin (*Neopelma aurifrons*); golden-crowned manakin (*Pipra vilasboasi*); yellow-headed manakin (*Chloropipo flavicapilla*).

DISTRIBUTION: Montane Atlantic forest – from 3,000–6,600ft (900–2,000m), mainly in areas dominated by Paraná pine (*Araucaria angustifolia*) and *Podocarpus lamberti* trees in southeastern Brazil, from the state of Rio de Janeiro south to the northern part of the state of Rio Grande do Sul; 1 confirmed record from northeastern Argentina.

SIZE: Length: 5in (12cm).

FORM: A small, large-headed bird with a short, thick, yellow bill, orange-yellow legs and feet, and reddish-brown and black plumage.

It has a black cap and nape, rich chestnut back, rump, and wing-coverts; the wings are black with yellow fringes and a yellow patch at the base of the flight feathers. The tail is chestnut with black central feathers; the face is buff grading into pale yellow. The female has an olive back and indistinct pale-grayish wing-bars.

DIET: Insects and other invertebrates; also fruit.

BREEDING: Details are not recorded; it may breed during the Southern hemisphere spring.

CONSERVATION: This attractive little bird's forest habitat has

suffered a great deal of destruction, firstly by gold and diamond mining, and more recently by clearance for coffee, banana, and rubber plantations. In the state of Paraná alone, an estimated 78 percent of the forest had been cut down by 1965, and the destruction continues. However, the bird is already protected in Brazil and is known to occur in at least four wildlife reserves. To improve its chances of survival, conservationists are searching for fresh sites where the birds may be living. If the species is found at many new sites, it may be taken off the IUCN's list of threatened animals.

BRAZIL BASED
The black-capped manakin is a rare bird now found only in mountain forests in southeastern Brazil. It is classed as Vulnerable because its numbers are known to be small and possibly declining.

BLUE BIRD OF PARADISE

Paradisaea rudolphi
Family: PARADISAEIDAE
Order: PASSERIFORMES

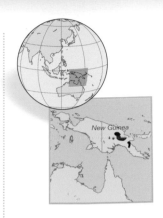

STATUS: Vulnerable (IUCN); CITES II. The population is estimated at fewer than 10,000 birds. Related endangered species: MacGregor's bird of paradise (*Macgregoria pulchra*); black sicklebird (*Epimachus fastuosus*); Wahne's parotia (*Parotia wahnesi*).

DISTRIBUTION: Mainly montane primary oak forest, forest edge, and older secondary growth at lower levels 4,600–5,900ft (1,400–1,800m) in Papua New Guinea, in mountains of eastern Central Ranges.

SIZE: Length: male 26in (67cm), including elongated tail feathers; female 12in (30cm). Weight: 4–7oz (124–189g).

FORM: Pigeon-sized bird with dark plumage, white eye-ring, and a stout, blue-white bill. The male has glossy black plumage with blue feathers on the wings, lower back, and tail, and long, gauzelike plumes.

The male's 2 central feathers in the tail are its chief distinguishing features (and are highly prized by poachers), forming long ribbons with spatula-shaped tips. The female lacks plumes and has chestnut underparts, but otherwise resembles the male.

DIET: Mainly fruit, including figs, wild peppers, and wild bananas; also insects, including crickets, and spiders.

BREEDING: A nest bowl built in a tree or bush; usually 1 pale-pink egg with lavender-gray and brown markings is laid and incubated by female for about 18 days; the young cared for by female alone.

CONSERVATION. The blue bird of paradise's habitat range lies entirely within the zone most favored in Papua New Guinea for new settlements, agriculture, and logging. There are existing protective laws and various public education programs are planned but threats remain. Hunting is one of them: the species is sought after by the islanders for its spectacular plumes, which are used in headdresses and other ritual jewellery. Where males are regularly hunted, they may abandon an area. These losses may be compounded by the blue bird's competition with the Raggiana bird of paradise, which is better able to adapt to disturbed habitat. Studies are planned into the effects of habitat change and hunting on its population.

HUNTED FOR FEATHERS
The male blue bird of paradise is hunted for its feathers (which are used in headdresses) whereas its stunning looks should help instead to publicize efforts to protect it.

137

BLUE SWALLOW

Hirundo atrocaerulea
Family: HIRUNDINIDAE
Order: PASSERIFORMES

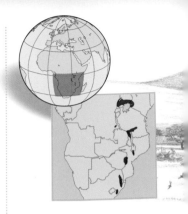

STATUS: Vulnerable (IUCN); not listed by CITES. About 3,000 birds remain. Another 4 species in the swallow and martin family are threatened, the most closely related being the white-tailed swallow (*Hirundo megaensis*).

DISTRIBUTION: Breeds in montane grassland in upland areas of southern Africa. Migrates to grassland and savanna, visiting northeastern Democratic Republic of the Congo, southern Uganda, and western Kenya.

SIZE: Length head/body: 7–10in (18–25cm); tail streamers of male: 4.8–5.5in (12–14cm), of female: (2.3–3in (6–8cm).

FORM: A slim swallow with long outer tail feathers (streamers) in the male; shorter in the female and short in juveniles. Adult plumage often looks all black, but in sunlight appears deep, glossy blue; the flight feathers are brownish black with a greenish-blue tinge.

DIET: Aerial insects; mainly flies.

BREEDING: Usually November–January; open-cup nest of mud and grass is built. The female lays 2–3 brown and purplish spotted white eggs. Young fledge at 20–26 days; usually a second brood is reared later in the breeding season.

CONSERVATION: The beautiful blue swallow has declined greatly in South Africa and Swaziland, where it is close to extinction, and in Zimbabwe and Zambia, where it is rare. The grassland in which it nests, breeds, and feeds is disappearing with the spread of commercial logging, sugarcane planting, and grass burning.

REARING WORRIES
The blue swallow
receives protection
within national parks or
nature reserves in
some areas. However,
there is an urgent need
to locate the birds' key
wintering sites and
preserve them.

GURNEY'S PITTA

Pitta gurneyi
Family: PITTIDAE
Order: PASSERIFORMES

STATUS: Critically Endangered (IUCN); CITES I. Probably fewer than 20 birds remain. Nine species of pitta are on threatened, like the superb pitta (*Pitta superba*) and whiskered pitta (*P. kochi*).

DISTRIBUTION: Secondary, regenerating, lowland semievergreen forest at just 1 site (Khao Nor Chuchi Sanctuary) in southern Thailand.

SIZE: Length: 8in (20cm). Weight: 2–3oz (60–90g).

FORM: A sturdy-bodied, large-headed, short-tailed bird with an upright posture and strong, longish legs. The male has a black forecrown and dark-blue nape; also red-brown wings and upperparts, yellow and black underparts, and a deep-blue tail. The female has red-brown upperparts and a blue tail, but has a buffy-brown crown and nape, blackish-brown eyepatch, whitish throat, and buff underparts with fine black barring.

DIET: Worms, insects and insect larvae, snails, slugs, and other small animals.

BREEDING: During the wet season, April–October. The nest is a dome of dead leaves and small sticks on a base of slightly larger sticks; the inner cup for eggs is lined with fine, black rootlets; usually 3–4 eggs are laid and incubated by both sexes for an unknown period, but probably 10–14 days; young fledge at 14–15 days.

CONSERVATION: This spectacular bird suffered as a result of the felling of Thailand's lowland forests for timber and for the cultivation of fruit, coffee, rubber, and palm oil.

TRAPPERS' DELIGHT
Gurney's pitta boasts spectacular plumage, making it irresistible to cage-bird trappers. Forest clearance, too, has caused a sharp decline in numbers, and the bird now faces extinction.

The birds have also been hunted and trapped in the country's illegal but thriving cage-bird trade. A conservation plan began in the 1980s to involve local people in management and education activities intended to reduce trapping and forest clearance. However, prices for rubber and palm oil fell and settlers planted fresh trees, destroying yet more established forest in the process.

HUIA

Heteralocha acutirostris
Family: CALLAEIDAE
Order: PASSERIFORMES

NEW ZEALAND

STATUS: Extinct (IUCN); not listed by CITES. Related endangered species: Kokako (*Callaeas cinerea*); saddleback (*Phiestrurnus carunclulatus*).

DISTRIBUTION: Formerly found in the lowland forests of North Island, New Zealand.

SIZE: Length head/body: 10–12in (25–30cm); tail: 7–9in (18–23cm).

FORM: A black, long-legged, slender, crowlike bird with orange wattles (loose folds of skin hanging from bill base). Differently curved beak on the male and female. White tip to the tail.

DIET: Insects, grubs, and worms found on forest floor and among rotting wood.

BREEDING: Little is known; 2–4 gray, brown, and purplish-spotted eggs laid October–November in a large cup-shaped nest of sticks and twigs lined with finer material.

CONSERVATION: The unique huia of New Zealand was revered by the local Maori people. They collected the distinctive white-tipped tail feathers but were careful not to kill too many birds. In the late 18th century, European settlers, finding it hard to make a living, found that the birds fetched good prices in museums and private collections. The birds were incredibly tame, having no natural predators, and proved easy to capture as they hopped along on the forest floor. The settlers also brought domestic animals that then became another threat to the huia. The birds' main problem, however, was loss of forest habitat and land clearances.

Its habitat – moist, warm forest with plenty of rotten wood – simply vanished. The huia had nowhere to feed. The last reliable report of a living huia was in 1907. There have been further claimed sightings, but none has been confirmed.

NOWHERE TO FEED
Protective legislation in 1892 came too late to save this New Zealand bird. Huias were famous as the only species of bird in which the male and female had different bills: the female's long, slender and curved, the male's thick and chisel-like.

143

MANGROVE FINCH

Camarhynchus heliobates
Family: EMBERIZIDAE
Order: PASSERIFORMES

STATUS: Critically endangered (IUCN); not listed by CITES. Probably fewer than 50 pairs remain. Related endangered species: olive-headed brush finch (*Atlapetes flaviceps*); multicolored tanager (*Chlorochrysa nitidissima*); Guadalupe junco (*Junco insularis*); Cochabamba mountain finch (*Poospiza garleppi*); Cuban sparrow (*Torreornis inexpectata*).

DISTRIBUTION: Dense mangrove forest at 2 sites in northwestern Isabela, Galápagos Islands, in the Pacific Ocean.

SIZE: Length: 5.5in (14cm). Weight: 0.6oz (18g).

FORM: Small brown finch with a strong, pointed bill. It has dull-brown upperparts with an olive rump; a pale, faintly dark-streaked breast. Male and female are alike.

DIET: Mainly insects and spiders, plus a small amount of vegetable matter.

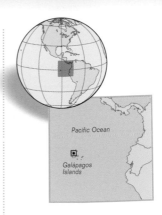

Pacific Ocean

Galápagos Islands

BREEDING: January–May (the rainy season). The male becomes territorial and builds several speculative dome-shaped nests in the mangroves, displaying to attract a female; after selecting a nest (or helping to build a better one) and mating, the female lays 2–5 eggs, incubating them for about 12 days. Some pairs rear more than 1 clutch (up to 5). The chicks are fed by both their parents and fledge at 13–14 days.

CONSERVATION: The mangrove finch lives among the forests of mangrove that grow in coastal shallows and around saltwater lagoons. The mangroves have been cut back and so has their habitat.

This finch is now restricted to less than half a square mile and its numbers are still dwindling. The decline may be due to introduced species, such as black rats that eat the birds' eggs and young. Wild cats, egg-stealing birds, and stinging fire ants are also problematic. Yet none of these is a proven threat, and the true reason for the bird's decline remains a mystery. Today the species is strictly protected, and research programs have been initiated to find out why the mangrove finch is still in decline.

DECLINING MYSTERY
The mangrove finch is being protected from predators and competitors. Through careful monitoring of the population, its main enemy may yet be revealed and its future assured.

145

MAURITIUS FODY

Foudia rubra
Family: PLOCEIDAE
Order: PASSERIFORMES

MADAGASCAR

MAURITIUS

Indian Ocean

STATUS: Critically Endangered (IUCN); not listed by CITES. Fewer than 250 birds exist. Thirteen other species in the weaverbird family are threatened, including 2 other species of fody: the Seychelles fody (*Foudia sechellarum*) and Rodrigues fody (*F. flavicans*).

DISTRIBUTION: Native forests in part of southwestern Mauritius, including those dominated by pines and degraded forest invaded by nonnative trees.

SIZE: Length: 5.5in (14cm).

FORM: A bird slightly smaller than a sparrow, with a large head, thick neck, plump body, and short tail; the male has a bright red head, neck, and breast with a small black patch between the eye and the bill; the back, wings, and tail are dark brown, streaked with buff; reddish rump and uppertail coverts (feathers covering base of upper tail). The female is much duller, mainly drab dark brown.

The male molts into a female-like plumage for a very short period in winter.

DIET: Insects; also fruit, nectar.

BREEDING: A nest of dried leaves, mosses, and plant fibers, well-lined with soft feathers and usually sited at the end of a branch is built mainly by the male; 3 pale blue eggs incubated for about 14 days; young fledge in about 18–20 days.

CONSERVATION: The colorful Mauritius fody is threatened due to the massive clearance of native upland forest in Mauritius. Introduced animals – deer, pigs, monkeys, black rats, giant African

snails, and many different insects –
destroy or compete with this native
species. Another factor is the
frequent occurence of cyclones
(tropical storms) that damage the
already degraded areas of forest.
Attempts to reverse the overall
decline of the fody population include
the setting up of a captive-breeding
program and the control of monkeys
and rats as part of a plan to restore
areas of native vegetation.

ISLAND HAVEN
The Mauritius fody
may be saved by the
setting up of a
Conservation
Management Area
on Mauritius where
predators are
controlled, and
nectar-producing
plants are introduced
to supply the birds
with food.

147

NIGHT PARROT

Geopsittacus occidentalis
Family: PSITTACIDAE
Order: PASSERIFORMES

Unverified
reports

STATUS: Critically Endangered (IUCN); CITES I and II. Population unknown, but perhaps fewer than 50 birds. Related endangered species: golden-shouldered parrot (*Psephotus chrysopterygius*); swift parrot (*Lathamus discolor*); orange-bellied parrot (*Neophema chrysogaster*).

DISTRIBUTION: Arid and semiarid plains of the Australian outback. Spinefex grassland or goosefoot and samphire shrublands on floodplains, claypans, or by watercourses or salt lakes; recently in rolling plains of Mitchell grass with scattered goosefoot shrubs.

SIZE: Length: 8.5–10in (22–25cm); wingspan: 17–18in (44–46cm).

FORM: A smallish parrot with a stocky build and a short tail. It is bright yellowish-green below the breast with dark mottling and barring except on the belly; the upper wing has dark-grayish flight feathers and a pale-yellow wingbar.

The underwing is grayish-green with a broader yellow wingbar.

DIET: Likely to feed on seeds of grasses and other plants.

BREEDING: Virtually unknown; the nest is described as being of small sticks or leaves in a clump of vegetation at the end of a tunnel or runway made in the soil; clutch may be 2–4 eggs, possibly up to 6.

CONSERVATION: The elusive night parrot has only been authentically recorded a handful of times since the 1880s, with most sightings remaining unconfirmed. There was, however, one authenticated sighting in 1990.

There have been unconfirmed reports of night parrot sightings from all the mainland states of Australia, so it is possible that the bird survives in low density over much of its former range. Threats are thought to include predation by nonnative mammals, especially wild cats and foxes. The birds may also suffer competition for food from cattle and other livestock, and rabbits. Their water supply may have been reduced by the spread of wild camels that were introduced into arid areas over 100 years ago for transporting people and goods. Locating a viable population is vital if this parrot is to be rescued. Captive-breeding programs could then be introduced, research done into the birds' ecology, and the damage caused by habitat degradation reversed.

PARROT PUZZLE
The night parrot is one of the world's least known and most rarely seen birds, and is thought to have a tiny population. Although sightings have become rarer, this parrot may not be currently declining.

PACIFIC ROYAL FLYCATCHER

Onychorhynchus occidentalis
Family: TYRANNIDAE
Order: PASSERIFORMES

ECUADOR

STATUS: Vulnerable (IUCN); not listed by CITES. Population of 2,500–10,000 birds. Related endangered species: Atlantic royal flycatcher (*Onychorhynchus swainsoni*).

DISTRIBUTION: Humid and deciduous lowland forests below 3,900ft (1,200m) in western Ecuador, from Esmeraldas Province south to El Oro Province, including the adjoining part of the Tumbes Department in northwestern Peru.

SIZE: Length: 6.3–6.5in (16–16.5cm). Weight: about 0.8oz (21g).

FORM: A sparrow-sized bird with a long, broad bill fringed with long bristles. A large crest normally held flat gives the head its hammerhead shape: the crest is sometimes erected to form a brightly colored fan. Both sexes have drab upperparts, unmarked apart from small buff spots on wing-coverts, chestnut rump, and tall, whitish throat; rest of the underparts are orange-buff. In the male the fan is mostly shiny scarlet with scattered black spots and feathers tipped with blue; in the female scarlet is replaced by orange-yellow.

DIET: Mainly large insects such as butterflies, bugs, and dragonflies caught in flight or in darting sallies from branch to branch.

BREEDING: The nest is a long, slender structure of plant fibers, rootlets, dry leaves, live epiphytes (plants that grow on other plants), and bits of moss suspended from a vine or branch high above a shaded stream, sheltered from the wind; 2 reddish-brown eggs are laid.

CONSERVATION: The flamboyantly crested Pacific royal flycatcher occurs exclusively in lowland forest, much of which, below an altitude of 2,900ft (900m), has already been felled for timber. Logging even threatens protected areas such as Ecuador's Cordillera de Molleturo Protection Forest. Grazing by goats and cattle in logged areas prevents trees from regenerating and clears the understory of the remaining forest. If this destruction continues or increases, the Pacific royal flycatcher's status may need to be revised to Endangered.

LOGGING OFF
Habitat loss from logging is making this distinctive bird Endangered rather than Vulnerable. Its magnificently colored fan, displayed at times of mating or preening, should make its conservation a priority.

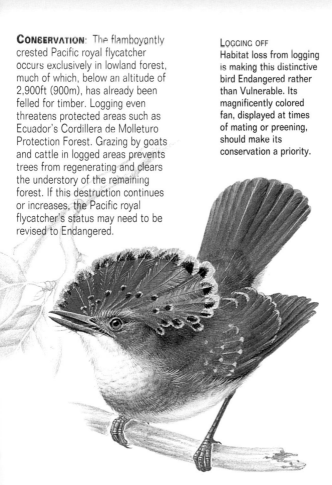

RED SISKIN

Caruelis cucullata
Family: FRINGILLIDAE
Order: PASSERIFORMES

STATUS: Endangered (IUCN); CITES I. About 250–1,000 individuals remain. Related endangered species: yellow-faced siskin (*Carduelis yarrellini*); saffron siskin (*C. siemiradzkii*); Warsangli linnet (*C. johannis*).

DISTRIBUTION: Moves seasonally and daily between moist evergreen forest, dry deciduous woodland, and adjacent shrubby grassland and pastureland. Recent sightings in 4 states in northern Venezuela. Population in northern Colombia and Puerto Rico.

SIZE: Length: 4in (10cm).

FORM: A small, brightly patterned red-and-black finch. The male has a jet-black head, chin, throat, and tail; also black wings with a broad red bar across flight feathers; rest of plumage is rich scarlet to pinkish red. Female is brownish gray from head to back; the crown, nape, and "shoulders" streaked darker; the rump and wingbars are orange-red.

DIET: Seeds of trees and shrubs; grass seeds, flower heads, and cactus fruit.

BREEDING: Main nesting season is May–early June; second breeding in November and December. Neat, cup-shaped nest built in tall trees.

CONSERVATION: The main reason for the beautiful red siskin's catastrophic decline has been trapping for the cage-bird trade. Since the 1940s trade in the birds has been illegal, but trapping continued on a massive scale for much of the last century. Large numbers went to breeders, who introduced the genes for red color (particularly prominent in the male)

into domestic canaries. Red siskins also face loss of habitat as a result of the spread of intensive agriculture. Captive-breeding programs have been initiated, but they have been beset by problems of disease and genetically impure stock. Estimates as to how many birds are left in the wild vary from a few thousand to several hundred.

CAGED BIRD
The red siskin has been brought to the verge of extinction chiefly as a result of the relentless demands of the cage-bird trade. There may be too few left in the wild to save from extinction.

153

REGENT HONEYEATER

Xanthomyza phrygia
Family: MELIPHAGIDAE
Order: PASSERIFORMES

AUSTRALIA

STATUS: Endangered (IUCN); not listed by CITES. About 1,500 birds remain. Many related endangered species including: Crow honeyeater (*Gymnomyza aubryana*); black-eared miner (*manorina melanotis*); stitchbird (*Notiomystis cincta*); dusky friarbird (*Philemon fuscicapillus*); painted honeyeater (*Grantiella picta*).

DISTRIBUTION: Dry, open forests and woodlands, especially those dominated by yellow box, red ironbark, and yellow gum trees in southeastern Australia; also riverside forests of river she-oaks in New South Wales.

SIZE: Length: 8–9.5in (20–24cm).

FORM: A slim-bodied bird with a downcurved, sharp-tipped bill and long tail. The male has a black head, neck, upper back, and upper breast, and a patch of bare, pink. or yellow skin around each eye; 3 broad yellow panels in each wing. The female is smaller and duller.

DIET: Nectar, insects, honeydew (sugary secretions of aphids and plant-eating insects), and fruit.

BREEDING: Mainly August–January; a nest of bark and plant strips lined with plant down and hair is built in a tree.

CONSERVATION: Fragmentation of the regent honeyeater's habitat seems to be favoring more aggressive species, such as the noisy miner, which may be replacing the honeyeater in parts of its range. Today only about a quarter of its habitat remains, the rest having been cleared for agriculture, timber, and other developments.

HARD TO ADAPT
Regent honeyeaters
have suffered loss of
their forest habitat,
and also lost out to
their more adaptable
rivals. Their habitat
must be monitored to
ensure that it is not
further degraded.

Conservationists carry out
annual surveys of the species'
range and abundance and a
captive colony has now been
established. Logging and
grazing have been restricted at
some major sites, and many of
the trees favored by the
honeyeater have been planted
to replace those destroyed.

WRITHED HORNBILL

Aceros leucocephalus
Family: BUCEROTIDAE
Order: BUCEROTIFORMES

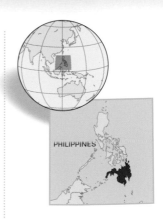

PHILIPPINES

STATUS: Lower Risk (IUCN); CITES II. Population of 10,000–20,000 birds. Many related endangered species include: Mindoro tarictic (*Penelopides mindorensis*); Narcondam hornbill (*Aceros narcondami*); plain-pouched hornbill (*A. subruficollis*).

DISTRIBUTION: Lowland and midaltitude rain forest in Mindanao and adjacent islands, Philippines.

SIZE: Length: 30in (76cm).

FORM: A large, rakish bird with a bright red bill and a bony casque. Red skin around eye and throat.

DIET: Mainly fruit; also large insects, reptiles, birds' eggs, and nestlings.

BREEDING: Female seals herself into a tree hole and then lays 1 to 3 eggs. The male feeds the female during incubation; the female breaks the seal at about 3 months, and the chicks fledge.

CONSERVATION: The writhed hornbill's home, chiefly the island of Mindanao in the Philippines, is threatened by logging, which destroys the largest trees on which the hornbills depend for nesting holes. The figure of 29 percent of the island covered by forest (1988) certainly no longer applies. The birds are also hunted and shot for their meat and taken as pets. Commercial logging is now mostly forbidden, but the land is being turned over to agriculture to feed the growing human population. The hornbill's survival will depend on lowland or hill forest conservation under the National Integrated Protected Areas System as well as education on sustainable hunting.

PHILIPPINES FOREST
The writhed hornbill
depends for its survival
on properly protected
areas of lowland or hill
forest. Its future may
be assured if the
Philippine eagle,
Mindanao's national
bird, is protected.

SALMON-CRESTED COCKATOO

Cacatua moluccensis
Family: PSITTACIDAE
Order: PSITTACIFORMES

STATUS: Vulnerable (IUCN), CITES I. Wild population down to fewer than 10,000 birds; 10,000 in captivity.

DISTRIBUTION: The forests and open woodland of the large, mountainous Indonesian Island of Seram and at one site on Ambon, one of Seram's three offshore islands; until recently, also on the other two, Saparua and Haruku.

SIZE: Length: 18–20in (46–52cm) including tail feathers. Female is slightly larger than the male.

FORM: Usually a pale salmon pink, sometimes white, with a large, backward-sweeping crest with deep-pink central feathers. The underwings are mostly a deep salmon pink, and the undertail is orange-pink.

DIET: Seeds, fruits, berries, and nuts. In plantations, green coconuts.

BREEDING: Little studied in the wild. It nests in tree hollows that it often extends with its powerful bill to as much as 15ft (4.5m). In captivity, it lays 2 eggs and incubates them for 4 weeks. Chicks stay in the nest for about 4 months.

CONSERVATION: Until the late 1970s, this beautiful cockatoo was common over most of its range, feeding and roosting in flocks of up to 16 birds. Today it survives in much smaller numbers – victim to extensive logging destroying its home and to trappers snaring the birds for their delicate plumage. Despite an export ban, trappers risk their lives climbing hundreds of feet into the forest canopy to catch the birds at their nest entrances. They sell the cockatoos for a few dollars to dealers who sell them on to smugglers.

DELICATE PINK PLUMAGE
The salmon-crested cockatoo's feathers have made it a prime target for the illegal cage-bird market – so much so that 20 years ago it was virtually extinct. Up to 50 birds a week continue to be snared.

Smugglers may get up to $2,500 on the illegal pet market – assuming the bird has survived the journey stuffed in a suitcase or a plastic pipe. But there is hope: an international-backed program of research and conservation has created income from canopy-viewing ecotourists and persuaded villagers to reject renewal of contracts with the logging companies.

BROWN KIWI

Apteryx mantelli
Family: APTERYGIDAE
Order: STRUTHIONIFORMES

NEW
ZEALAND

STATUS: Endangered (IUCN); not listed by CITES. About 35,000 birds survive. Related endangered species: Great spotted kiwi (*Apteryx haastii*); little spotted kiwi (*A. owenii*); tooeka (*A. australis*).

DISTRIBUTION: Subtropical and temperate forests; regenerating forest, shrubland, pine plantations, and pastureland in North Island, New Zealand. Isolated population on Okarito, South Island, New Zealand may be a separate species with Critical status.

SIZE: Length: 16in (40cm). Weight: male 3–6.5lb (1.4–3kg); female 4.5–8lb (2–3.8kg).

FORM: A bird the size of a small dog; it has a small head; a long, slightly downcurved bill with bristles at the base and a long neck (usually drawn in); rotund body covered with coarse, hairlike plumage, gray-brown with red-brown streaks. The kiwi has strong legs with 4 toes on each foot.

DIET: Invertebrates in soil and leaf litter, especially earthworms, spiders, and insects; also fruit, seeds, and leaves.

BREEDING: The female lays 1 or 2 very large eggs in August – September in a burrow or natural cavity; egg(s) incubated by the male for 11–12 weeks; chick(s) independent at 14–20 days.

CONSERVATION: The unique brown kiwi was never under threat until the mid-19th century, when European settlers hunted the birds for their plumage. A law banning the hunting, capture, or killing of kiwis was passed in New Zealand in 1908.

However, land clearance for agriculture and settlements destroyed much of their forest habitat. The birds' fate was further sealed when predatory mammals such as cats, dogs, and stoats were introduced. These remain the principal threat facing the brown kiwi – predators kill half of all kiwi chicks before they reach breeding age. Conservationists have an accurate picture of kiwi populations thanks to a national program of monitoring, but continued protection is vital.

NEW ZEALAND PROTECTION
The brown kiwi lays a huge egg. Each chick has only a 50 percent chance of survival. To protect the species, predators are culled and chicks hand-reared to an age when they can fend off attacks.

DODO

Raphus cucullatus
Family: RAPHIDAE
Order: COLUMBIFORMES

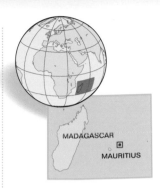

MADAGASCAR

MAURITIUS

STATUS: Extinct (IUCN); not listed by CITES.

DISTRIBUTION: Lived in lowland forests of Mauritius, Indian Ocean.

SIZE: Length: about 30in (75cm). Weight: up to 50lb (23kg).

FORM: A gray, turkey-sized bird, often depicted as plump (though probably not as rounded as depicted in illustrations). It had large, fleshy feet, a tuft of white tail feathers, and a thick, long bill measuring 9in (20cm) with a hooked tip. It was a ground dweller with stubby, flightless wings.

DIET: Large quantities of fruit gathered from forest floor, perhaps supplemented by invertebrates, including snails and worms.

BREEDING: Believed to lay a single white egg on the ground.

CONSERVATION: The dodo was a kind of giant ground pigeon.

It lived on the island of Mauritius, an island that had no native mammals and no human inhabitants, so this flightless bird could nest on the ground and roam around without risk.

Portuguese navigators discovered the dodo in about 1507. The sailors found the birds easy to catch and kill and would stock up on fresh meat before continuing their travels. Eventually Mauritius was colonized by the French and then the British, who cleared the forests to make way for sugarcane, and imported pigs, monkeys, cats, and dogs; with them also came rats. The introduced animals were highly effective scavengers and predators. Although the adult dodos could defend themselves, their eggs were swiftly gobbled up.

The fruit trees that provided a vital part of their diet vanished, and within about 155 years of its discovery, the dodo was extinct. Indeed, no dodos were found during a visit to Mauritius in 1682. The dodo has since become an international symbol for extinction and a reminder of the pressures facing wildlife in the modern world. The expression "dead as a dodo" has even entered our language to describe something that is dead or defunct. Studies of dodo bones indicate it might have been slimmer than the commonly depicted plump fowl.

DEAD AS A DODO
The dodo was first discovered in about 1507, yet by 1682 it no longer existed. Few people ever saw a dodo alive, but it has since become world famous as a symbol of extinction.

KAGU

Rhynochetos jubatus
Family: RHYNOCHETIDAE
Order: GRUIFORMES

STATUS: Endangered (IUCN); CITES I. Probably no more than 800 individuals exist.

DISTRIBUTION: Mainly lowland rain forest and drier mountain forest in New Caledonia, a Pacific (French-ruled) island. Also lives in closed-canopy scrub during wet season.

SIZE: Length: 22in (55cm); wingspan: 31in (78cm).

FORM: A plump-bodied bird with orange-red bill and legs. Its plumage is ash gray and white, darker above, with long feathers extending from the nape to form a crest. Broad wings show a barred pattern on open flight feathers.

DIET: Worms, snails, lizards; also cockroaches, beetles, spiders.

BREEDING: Adults build a ground nest of leaves; the female lays 1 creamy-brown egg. Parents share incubation and care of the chicks. Adults may pair for life.

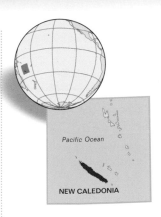

Pacific Ocean

NEW CALEDONIA

CONSERVATION: Since the French colonized New Caledonia in the 18th century, the flightless kagus have faced increasing threats. They have become easy prey to dogs and feral pigs, and rats. Over the years the kagu's forest habitats have dwindled to about 20 percent of their original size, due to fires, logging, and mining. New Caledonia also has some of the world's worst erosion problems. Road building, along with deforestation, makes it easy for dogs to enter undisturbed areas. However, there are signs that the bird may survive. Kagu numbers have increased steadily in one national park and they have bred readily in captivity, too.

NATIONAL EMBLEM
The kagu has been adopted as the official national emblem of New Caledonia. The bird's survival is important, since it draws wildlife watchers, who in turn boost the local economy.

MADAGASCAR RED OWL

Tyto soumagnei
Family: TYTONIDAE
Order: STRIGIFORMES

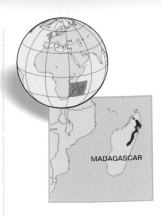

MADAGASCAR

STATUS: Endangered (IUCN); CITES I and II. About 1,000–2,500 birds remain. Related endangered species: Congo bay owl (*Podilus origoginei*); Minahasa masked owl (*Tyto inexspectata*); Taliabu masked owl (*T. nigrobrunnea*).

DISTRIBUTION: Primary evergreen rainforest; also human-altered, forest-edge habitats in Madagascar.

SIZE: Length: 11–12in (27.5–30cm). Weight: about 11.3oz (320g).

FORM: A medium-sized owl, similar to a barn owl but smaller, with orange-red plumage, dark above and pale below; the facial disk is tinged gray-buff, darker round the eyes and fringed with orange; the crown, upperparts, and underparts speckled with black dots; tail faintly barred. Juveniles similar to adults.

DIET: Small native mammals; also rats and possibly frogs.

BREEDING: The only recorded nest was 75ft (23m) above ground in a tree hollow; probably 2 eggs in a clutch (in radio-tagged owl 2 young fledged at 10 weeks); young stay in area of nest for at least 4 months.

CONSERVATION: Until recently, there had only been one confirmed sighting of the Madagascar red owl (in 1973). However, in the 1990s a number of the owls were seen at six different sites and one was radio-tagged. This enabled ornithologists to gather information about its behavior. It is now thought that the owls occur in all the remaining blocks of forest in northeast Madagascar – large enough to support a population.

The owls face severe threats from the continued destruction of their habitat, with native trees being replaced by trees that are unsuitable for the owl. The loss of forest also affects the owl's native mammal prey and thus the owl itself. It is hoped that future surveys of the owl population will show that the bird is less rare than presently feared. The protection provided by national parks and other reserves remains the best hope for the species' survival.

RARE SIGHTINGS
The red Madagascar owl lives in humid rain forests, which are now being rapidly destroyed. It is hoped that new research will reveal that the bird is not quite as rare as was once feared.

PHILIPPINE EAGLE

Pithecophaga jefferyi
Family: ACCIPITRIDAE
Order: FALCONIFORMES

PHILIPPINES

STATUS: Critically Endangered (IUCN); CITES I. 350–650 birds remain; possibly only around 220 mature adults. Related endangered species: New Guinea harpy eagle (*Harpyopsis novaeguineae*); harpy eagle (*Harpia harpyja*).

DISTRIBUTION: Primary hardwood rain forest on steep slopes on 4 Philippine islands; sometimes lives among secondary growth and gallery forest along riverbanks and floodplains.

SIZE: Length: 34–40in (86–102cm). Wingspan: about 6.5ft (2m). Weight: 10.3–17.6lb (4.7–8kg).

FORM: A huge eagle with a large, arched, powerfully hooked blue bill. Dark areas around the eyes (which have pale blue-gray irises) contrast with a buff crown and nape. Long, spiky, black-streaked feathers form a scruffy crest; cheeks, throat, underparts, and underwings are white; upperparts and upperwings dark brown; legs and feet yellow.

DIET: Tree-dwelling mammals such as flying lemurs, palm civets, monkeys, and flying squirrels; also tree-dwelling birds, including hornbills, owls, and hawks; bats, monitor lizards, and snakes.

BREEDING: The female lays 1 egg in stick nest in canopy of tall tree. Eaglet is dependent on its parents for a year or more after fledging.

CONSERVATION: As with so many endangered species, the main threat facing the Philippine eagle is the relentless destruction of its habitat. Every year some of the remaining primary forest is felled for timber. When the loggers leave, settlers who practice "slash-and-burn" cultivation move in, replacing trees with bamboo and scrub that is of little value to the eagles. Other threats include hunting by local people for food or trophies and, until recently, the capture of young for sale to zoos and the cage-bird trade. Over the past 40 years conservation initiatives have been launched but the work is hampered by the difficult nature of the eagle's remote habitat.

RARE BIRD OF PREY
The Philippine eagle, one of the world's rarest birds of prey, is in a precarious situation. Plans for its conservation include a campaign to foster national pride for the bird.

STELLER'S SEA-EAGLE

Haliaeetus pelagicus
Family: ACCIPITRIDAE
Order: FALCONIFORMES

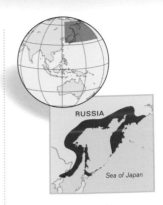

RUSSIA

Sea of Japan

STATUS: Vulnerable (IUCN); CITES I and II. Population is estimated at 5,000 birds. Related endangered species: Gray-headed fish-eagle (*Ichthyophaga ichthyaetus)*; lesser fish-eagle (*I. humilis*); Madagascar fish-eagle (*Haliaeetus vociferoides*); Pallas's sea-eagle (*H. leucoryphus*); Sanford's fish-eagle (*H. sanford*); white-tailed eagle (*H. albicilla*).

DISTRIBUTION: Breeds only on Kamchatka Peninsula, coasts around Sea of Okhotsk, lower reaches of River Amur, and Sakhalin and Shantar islands. Nests in mature trees or cliffs. Birds wintering in Russia stay mainly on coasts; those wintering in Japan stay near coasts or fresh water; some move to mountains.

SIZE: Length: 33.5–37in (85–94cm); wingspan: 7.2–8ft (2.2–2.5m).

FORM: A huge eagle with a massive, hooked, orange-yellow bill. It has blackish-brown plumage

except for white shoulders, forehead, thighs, rump, and a wedge-shaped tail. Its legs and feet are orange-yellow.

DIET: Living or dead fish, especially salmon; birds, mammals.

BREEDING: A huge nest of sticks, usually high up in tree or on a cliff; the female lays 2 white eggs.

CONSERVATION: Major worries include hydroelectric power projects and proposed offshore petro-chemical exploitation, which will affect the bird's food supply. In its Russian breeding grounds logging for timber threatens it too. Many of the tall, mature trees that the eagles use for nesting have been logged for timber, while pesticides and industrial pollutants do further damage.

On Hokkaido Island, Japan, where most of the eagles winter, over-fishing has caused serious declines in fish stocks. This has led to eagles wintering inland, where they eat carcasses of sika deer abandoned by hunters, and are often poisoned by the lead shot that killed the deer. Feeding stations have now been set up to deter the sea-eagles from consuming the contaminated deer.

FROM RUSSIA TO JAPAN Steller's sea-eagle may only be saved by measures to preserve its food sources, such as protecting the salmon spawning rivers and managing fish stocks in a sustainable way.

CALIFORNIA CONDOR

Gymnogyps californianus
Family: CATHARTIDAE
Order: FALCONIFORMES

STATUS: Critically Endangered (IUCN); CITES I and II. Population of around 200 birds, including those in the wild. Related endangered species: Andean condor (*Vultur gryphus*).

DISTRIBUTION: Rocky, open scrubland, coniferous forests, and oak savanna in southwestern U.S. Birds have been reintroduced in 3 areas in California and 2 in northern Arizona.

SIZE: Length: 46–54in (117–134cm).

FORM: A huge bird of prey; mostly black with white wing-linings and a silvery panel on upper secondaries. The head is naked and orange-red. Juveniles have black heads and dark mottling on the underwing.

DIET: Scavenges the carcasses of large mammals.

BREEDING: It nests in cavities in cliffs, rocky outcrops, large trees. Adapted for low reproduction rate.

CONSERVATION: Throughout the last century, the California Condor's range declined; in addition many birds were shot and killed, while others were poisoned by lead shot used to kill the animals on whose carcasses the eagles feasted. Since 1987, when the last remaining six wild individuals were captured, a large-scale integrated breeding and reintroduction program has been in operation. More than 50 birds have been reintroduced to the wild at several sites. However, the released birds have not found it easy to readapt to conditions in the wild. The $40m conservation program produced its first wild-born chick in 2002.

RESCUE PLANS
The California condor
rescue plan includes
establishing 15 breeding
pairs at two sites. Key
factors are the mainte-
nance of the birds' habitat,
and raising awareness of
the condor's plight.

ALABAMA RED-BELLIED TURTLE

Pseudemys alabamensis
Family: EMYDIDAE
Order: TESTUDINATA

Gulf of Mexico

STATUS: Endangered (IUCN); not listed by CITES. Unknown population. Related endangered species: Rio Grande cooter (*Pseudemys gorzugi*); American red-bellied turtle (*P. rubriventris*).

DISTRIBUTION: Scattered areas of freshwater streams and rivers with muddy bottoms running into Mobile Delta, Alabama.

SIZE: Length: females 13in (33.5cm); males 11in (29.5cm).

FORM: The shell has yellow and black eye spots on the scutes (shields). The carapace (upper shell covering the back) is green; the lower shell is orange; the colors darken with age. Head and limbs are brown with yellow stripes.

DIET: Aquatic plants; captive specimens take fish, meat, and earthworms.

BREEDING: One clutch per year of 3–9 eggs is laid.

CONSERVATION: Alabama red-bellied turtles have many natural predators such as alligators, the fish crow, racoons, and large fish. However, humans have by far caused the greatest downturn in their numbers. The red-belly once had a wider range, but urban development, drainage, and other human activity have restricted their territory. Waterside sites with loose, sandy soil are essential for the turtles to lay their eggs, and many such areas have been destroyed by off-road vehicles. In 1987 the the U.S. Fish and Wildlife service designated this turtle an endangered species, yet in spite of legal protection, the red-belly remains highly vulnerable.

The chief threats to its reliance on clean water and sandy beaches are pollution, pesticides, and lowering water levels, as well as the introduction of plants that choke the waterways. In addition, the turtles are collected for the pet trade, while the export of live turtles is not prohibited in the U.S.

TRADED AS PETS
The Alabama red-bellied turtle is an endangered species. Yet these semiaquatic creatures are still taken as pets by people who don't know how to take care of them.

GALÁPAGOS GIANT TORTOISE

Geochelone nigra
Family: TESTUDINIDAE
Order: TESTUDINATA

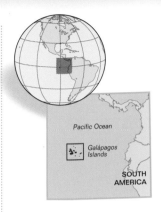

Pacific Ocean

Galápagos
Islands

SOUTH
AMERICA

STATUS: Vulnerable (IUCN); CITES I. About 10,000 remain. Related endangered species: All subspecies of *geochelone nigra* are on the IUCN Red List.

DISTRIBUTION: Galápagos Islands, which are hot, dry and volcanic with rocky outcrops; some forested areas with grassy patches.

SIZE: Length: up to 4ft (1.2m). Weight: up to 500lb (227kg).

FORM: A huge tortoise with a gray-brown shell and hard-scaled legs; some have domed shells; others are saddleback (resembling a saddle in shape).

DIET: Almost any green vegetation.

BREEDING: About 7–20 eggs are buried in soil.

CONSERVATION: There were once huge numbers of giant tortoises on the Galápagos Islands.

When settlers came to the islands in the 1830s, they brought pigs, goats, dogs, cattle, and donkeys. Some of these escaped and began to eat tortoise eggs and hatchlings, destroying vegetation and trampling tortoise nests. Rats and fire ants, both introduced species, also eat large numbers of hatchlings. Tortoises were also collected and taken to zoos all over the world. These Galápagos islands are now a national park, with laws preventing the removal of any animals. Some believe the islands may need 100 years to recover their vegetation and tortoise populations. The recovery program has included incubating eggs and breeding young artificially.

This has been successful, and in 2000, the 1000th bred tortoise was released onto one of the islands. The tortoise population has almost doubled in recent years, and laws have been passed to restrict settlement and protect the coastal waters, while quarantine laws forbid the introduction of nonnative plants and animals. One persistent problem is that groups of tortoises have been reduced to such low numbers on some islands that their lack of genetic diversity is a cause for concern.

MANY THREATS
The Galápagos giant tortoise is now rare or extinct on many of the islands because of the destruction of habitat and the introduction of animals that prey on the young or compete with adults for food.

HAWKSBILL TURTLE

Eretmochelys imbricata
Family: CHELONIIDAE
Order: TESTUDINATA

STATUS: Critically Endangered (IUCN); CITES I. Unknown worldwide population. All other sea turtles are related endangered species.

DISTRIBUTION: Shallow, tropical and subtropical seas, coral reefs, mangrove bays and estuaries of the Atlantic, Pacific, and Indian Oceans.

SIZE: Length: female 24–37in (62–94cm); male up to 39in (99cm).

FORM: An oval shell with a serrated (toothed) edge and a dark pattern on an amber background; paddlelike limbs.

DIET: Sponges and mollusks; also algae.

BREEDING: Nesting takes place only on sandy beaches. Up to 140 eggs per clutch are laid, usually overnight; 4–5 clutches per season; 2–3 years between breedings.

CONSERVATION: The hawksbill and other sea turtles have always been exploited for food, oil, and skins. But the pressure of human activity over the last 50 years has resulted in all sea turtle species becoming endangered. For many years the hawksbill's attractively colored shell has been the main source of tortoiseshell. Japan has been the largest user and although a member of CITES, Japan did not ban shell imports until 1993.

Turtle meat and eggs are still consumed in many countries, while turtle souvenirs are openly traded. Hawksbills have been recorded on the coasts of at least 96 countries, though in some of their former haunts the species is now thought to be extinct. Hawksbill females are in particular danger when they lay their eggs, a process that can take up to three hours. During this time, the turtles and their eggs are vulnerable to predators, including humans.

Hawksbills take at least 30 years to mature, a long time when you are trying to replenish your population. Another problem is that nesting beaches have facilities for tourists built on them. Beach raking destroys nests, while offroad vehicles compact the sand, crushing eggs. Artificial lighting attracts hatchlings that would otherwise head for the light on the horizon at sea, and they die of dehydration or are attacked by predators.

CHINESE ALLIGATOR

Alligator sinensis
Family: ALLIGATORIDAE
Order: CROCODILIA

STATUS: Critically Endangered (IUCN); CITES I. About 1,000 adults are left in the wild. Related endangered species: black caiman (*Melanosuchus niger*).

DISTRIBUTION: Slow-moving freshwater rivers and streams, and lakes, ponds, and swamps in the lower Yangtze River in China.

SIZE: Length: up to 6ft (2m). Weight: up to 85lb (40kg).

FORM: Similar to the American alligator, but smaller and with a more tapered head. The snout is slightly upturned near the nostrils. The color is dark brown to black. The young carry bright-yellow crossbands that fade with age.

DIET: Snails, mussels, fish, and ducks.

BREEDING: A clutch of 10–40 eggs per year are laid under mounds of decaying vegetation. The average clutch size in captivity is 15 eggs.

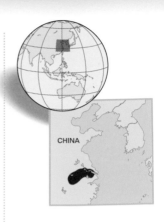

CHINA

RAREST ALLIGATOR? the Chinese alligator is one of the smaller crocodilians, and possibly the rarest. Its survival in the wild depends on a change in people's attitudes and greater protection of the animal's habitat.

Females may occasionally miss breeding one year. The incubation period is about 70 days. The young live together up to the age of 3 or 4 years, but as they grow fights and cannibalism can be a problem. Females mature at between 4 and 5 years, making them ideal for captive breeding rescue programs.

CONSERVATION: Once widespread, the Chinese alligator is now mainly restricted to 13 small protected areas within one nature reserve. The alligators' habitat is in an area of dense human population that has been heavily cultivated, principally by draining swamps and clearing vegetation. The Chinese alligator is not a man-eater. However, it is feared by local people and considered a nuisance because of its burrowing, which destroys irrigation dams. It is a protected species, but that does not stop it being killed and sold for meat and eastern medicines.

Captive-breeding programs have been successful and there are now more than 5,000 alligators in establishments in China – that is, there are more Chinese alligators in captivity than in the wild. Outside China over 200 exist in zoos. The alligator's long life and large clutch size mean that wild areas could be repopulated if the habitat was not constantly threatened.

GHARIAL

Gavialis gangeticus
Family: GAVIALIDAE
Order: CROCODILIA

STATUS: Endangered (IUCN); CITES I. Fewer than 2,500 remain.

DISTRIBUTION: Calmer areas of deep rivers, with sandbanks for nesting in north India and Nepal.

SIZE: Length: male 19–22ft (6–7m); female about 16ft (5m).

FORM: Just like a crocodile but with an elongated, narrow snout. This holds many interlocking, sharp teeth. The males have a bulbous growth on the end of the snout. Adult color is uniform olive gray, sometimes with brownish blotches or bands, especially on the tail.

DIET: Fish, small mammals, frogs.

BREEDING: A clutch of 30–50 eggs is buried in loose sand; the eggs take 12–13 weeks to hatch.

CONSERVATION: The gharial was once found in the major rivers and their tributaries in the northern part of the Indian subcontinent. Today, the remaining populations are in India and Nepal, with perhaps a few specimens in isolated areas. The animal's decline has been due to human activity. Settlements along the rivers have destroyed or disturbed breeding areas, and fishermen do not like gharials as they compete for fish and destroy fishing nets. Gharials are also believed by local people to scavenge on corpses placed in the Ganges during funeral ceremonies. In some areas people hunt gharials for their meat, while the eggs and body parts are used in traditional eastern medicine. A recovery plan to prevent poaching was set up in India in the 1970s. Nine protected areas were established along the Ganges and its tributaries, and six captive-breeding and ranching centers were started. Several thousand young gharials have been released into the wild. This has steadied the decline in some areas. At smaller sites numbers have not increased since youngsters do not always remain in the release area. In Nepal, captive breeding and releases have produced only small improvements in numbers. The gharial is still rare in both India and Nepal and remains at risk from destruction of its habitat, and by human intervention through fishing and hunting.

There is a shortage of suitable release sites, and the high cost of captive breeding and protection is also a problem. Ideally, youngsters should not be released until they are about five years old. However, the cost of feeding and caring for them means that some have been released early, which reduces their chances of survival in the wild.

RARE IN INDAN RIVERS
The gharial, one of the largest crocodilian species, came close to extinction in the 1970s. Conservation programs have increased numbers, but its future still looks uncertain.

FLAT-TAILED HORNED LIZARD

Phrynosoma m'callii
Family: IGUANIDAE
Order: SQUAMATA

USA

Pacific Ocean

STATUS: Lower Risk (IUCN); not listed by CITES. Population unknown. Many members of the family Iguanidae are related endangered species.

DISTRIBUTION: Arid desert scrubland in southeastern California, southwestern Arizona into northern Sonora, Mexico, and Baja California.

SIZE: Length: 4–5in (11–14cm).

FORM: A flattened body with short spines and tubercules (domelike projections) on the back; 1 or 2 fringes of short, pointed, platelike scales along each side. There are spiny horns on the head. Coloration is pale gray, reddish brown, buff, and dark brown.

DIET: Mainly ants; also other insects.

BREEDING: Between 3 and 7 eggs are laid; possibly more than 1 clutch is produced per year.

CONSERVATION: The flat-tailed horned lizard has survived for millions of years in harsh desert areas, where temperatures can reach over 110°F (43°C). Its range once extended farther than today, but fragmentation and destruction of its habitat over many years have gradually squeezed it into a smaller area that is still being destroyed.

Large parts of its range have been converted for crop-growing, and the construction of irrigation ditches has fragmented the lizard's range. With agriculture come pesticides, which destroy the ants and other insects on which the lizards feed, as well as killing the lizards themselves. Roads also take their toll.

BANNED AS PETS
Flat-tailed horned lizards have long been popular pets and in many areas were collected and sold in their thousands, but the trade is now illegal in most US states.

A warm road surface offers ideal basking conditions for reptiles – which regulate their body temperature by sunbathing – but with fatal results. The spread of housing brings domestic pet and wild animal predators attracted by trash dumps. As human settlement spreads farther into the desert, more areas are used for off-road vehicles, which disturb the lizards' nests and kill the occupants, too. Though they do enjoy some protection – their collection and sale without a permit is banned – people still ignore the law.

GILA MONSTER

Heloderma suspectum
Family: HELODERMATIDAE
Order: SQUAMATA

STATUS: Vulnerable (IUCN); CITES II. Unknown population. Related endangered species: Mexican beaded lizard (*Heloderma horridum*).

DISTRIBUTION: Desert and semiarid regions of southwestern U.S. and western Mexico (Sonoran, Chihuahan, and Mojave Deserts), in sand, gravel, rocks, and vegetation such as saguaro, cholla, and prickly pear. It often shelters in the burrows of other animals.

SIZE: Length: 18–24in (45–60cm).

FORM: Heavy-bodied with a short, fat tail used to store fat, and short, powerful limbs for digging. The black face has glands in either side of lower jaw that contain venom; scales are small and beadlike; the coloration and pattern vary: black, orange, yellow, and pink markings in bars, spots, or blotches.

DIET: Eggs, small mammals, and birds.

BREEDING: One clutch of up to 12 eggs is laid.

CONSERVATION: One of the world's only two venomous lizards, the Gila monster's habitat has been reduced by urban development, agriculture, and industry in desert areas. Construction work, use of off-road vehicles, and other human activities, destroy the burrows where the Gila monster spends much of its time, particularly during the cold winter months. Deliberate killing of the Gila – out of fear, bravado, or ignorance – has taken its toll. Gilas are also increasingly kept as pets. Many have been taken from the wild, even though it is now illegal to do so. Some towns also have local laws against keeping Gilas. The species is listed on CITES Appendix II, which means that only Gilas bred in captivity can be exported. There has been pressure to upgrade Gilas to

Appendix I to legislate against any trade in the species. In some areas only authorized people can handle "nuisance" Gilas. There are guidelines on where they can then be released, so that they are not left in unsuitable habitats. Some areas of habitat are now reserves, and many zoos have groups, although not all are able to breed. Since captive-breeding is possible, numbers can be increased, but habitat loss remains a problem.

HOPE IN VENOM
The Gila monster's venom contains a substance that can be used in the treatment of diabetes. It is hoped that this discovery will ensure the survival of this unique species.

IBIZA WALL LIZARD

Podarcis pityusensis
Family: LACERTIDAE
Order: SQUAMATA

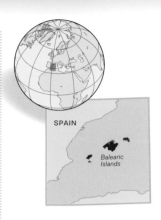

SPAIN

Balearic
Islands

STATUS: Vulnerable (IUCN); CITES II. Population unknown. Related endangered species: Lilford's wall lizard (*Podarcis lilfordi*); Miles wall lizard (*P. milensis*).

DISTRIBUTION: Dry, rocky areas with some plant cover in Balearic Islands, Spain; sometimes found in stone walls and ruined buildings.

SIZE: Length varies on each island, but average 6–8in (15–20cm).

FORM: Colors and shapes vary on each island. "Large island" lizards are mostly green on the back with light lines along the sides interspersed with spots or streaks. "Small island" populations may be melanistic (lacking light pigments), veering to black, dark brown, or dark blue, often with a dorsal pattern.

DIET: Mainly insects, some small invertebrates; sometimes young geckos or their own young; fruit, berries, and nectar.

BREEDING: Possibly 2 clutches per year of 2–6 eggs are laid.

CONSERVATION: The attractive Ibiza wall lizard was a favorite with collectors, who ranged from vacationers and reptile enthusiasts taking home a few specimens, to those operating on a commercial scale. Under Spanish law collecting lizards is illegal, but the law is not always rigorously enforced. The growth of tourism on the Balearic Islands, which now accounts for 80 percent of the islands' income, has destroyed much of the lizards' former habitat.

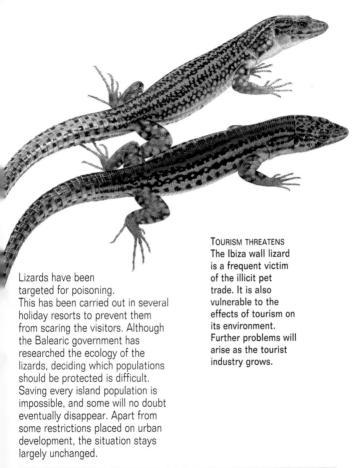

Lizards have been
targeted for poisoning.
This has been carried out in several
holiday resorts to prevent them
from scaring the visitors. Although
the Balearic government has
researched the ecology of the
lizards, deciding which populations
should be protected is difficult.
Saving every island population is
impossible, and some will no doubt
eventually disappear. Apart from
some restrictions placed on urban
development, the situation stays
largely unchanged.

TOURISM THREATENS
The Ibiza wall lizard
is a frequent victim
of the illicit pet
trade. It is also
vulnerable to the
effects of tourism on
its environment.
Further problems will
arise as the tourist
industry grows.

South Central Lesser Chameleon

Furcifer minor
Family: CHAMAELEONIDAE
Order: SQUAMATA

STATUS: Vulnerable (IUCN); CITES II. Unknown population. Related endangered species: Labord's chameleon (*Furcifer labordi*); Madagascar forest chameleon (*F. campani*).

DISTRIBUTION: Remaining areas of dry savanna forests in the southern part of central Madagascar.

SIZE: Length head/body: male up to 9in (23.7cm); female up to 6in (15.7cm).

FORM: The male is light to reddish brown with scattered darker brown patches and a few diagonal light bands on the body. The back part of the body carries a brown-edged white stripe of 2 spots on each side. The female is light green, but 2 violet spots and a few yellowish streaks are often present.

DIET: Insects.

BREEDING: Clutch of 11–16 eggs; 2–3 clutches per year.

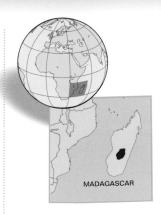

MADAGASCAR

Eggs are buried in soft soil and leaf litter; incubation lasts 9–10 months.

CONSERVATION: Problems facing the south central lesser chameleon are common to many animal and plant species on Madagascar, one of the world's poorest countries. The chameleon's IUCN listing is based on reduction in numbers, habitat loss, and possible threats from exploitation such as collecting for sale. Land clearance for agriculture and overgrazing by cattle have also denuded many areas, causing soil erosion and habitat destruction. Over the past few decades, national parks and reserves have been established on Madagascar. However, protection is not guaranteed. Unless Madagascar's economy improves, people will continue to clear the land to make a living, and the few cents earned by selling a lizard to a dealer are often desperately needed. Since 1995, export of all but four species of Madagascar's chameleons has been banned by the CITES committee. If the ban stays, this chameleon may survive because of its fairly high reproductive rate. However, it also depends critically on the protection of its habitat.

SAVANNA FOREST PROTECTION
The reptile's scarcity makes it especially vulnerable while its habitat comes under threat. South central lesser chameleons have striking differences in coloration between the light-green female (below) and the reddish brown male.

JAMAICAN BOA

Epicrates subflavus
Family: BOIDAE
Order: SQUAMATA

JAMAICA

STATUS: Vulnerable (IUCN); CITES I. Unknown population. Related endangered species: Cuban tree boa (*Epicrates angulifer*); Puerto Rican boa (*E. inornatus*); Virgin islands boa (*E. monensis granti*); Mona Island boa (*E. monensis monensis*).

DISTRIBUTION: Jamaican forests on honeycomb limestone; also on the island's moist, tropical forest areas. Safest population in the Blue Mountains in Portland, eastern Jamaica, and the Cockpit Country in Trelawny, to the north.

SIZE: Length: 6–8ft (1.8–2.4m).

FORM: A long, slender snake with a broad head; back part of the body yellowish tan or orange to reddish brown, black spots become irregular dark bands in the middle of the body. The posterior part of body is blue to black with irregular markings; a short dark stripe behind each eye. Males have pelvic spurs either side of the excretory cavity.

DIET: Mainly mammals such as rodents and bats, also birds; young feed mainly on lizards.

BREEDING: The 5–40 young have orange bodies with dark orange to brown crossbands; adult coloration develops at about 28 months.

CONSERVATION: Since the Spanish settled in Jamaica in the 15th century, the Jamaican boa has lost out to land being cleared for agriculture. Farmers brought pigs, goats, cats, and dogs, and these attracted rats. Mongoose were introduced to control the rats, and they preyed on the boas. Mining and tourism now also encroach on the snake's habitat. There are still remote, forested areas where the boa thrives, but more roads are being built, giving access to humans. Like many snakes, the nonvenomous Jamaican boa is often killed out of fear. Boas are successfully being bred in zoos and they are known to live for over 20 years in captivity and to produce sizable litters under these conditions. This should provide a good supply of young boas for reintroduction into the wild. However, the Jamaican boa's protection is still inadequate.

LEARNING TO COEXIST
The Jamaican boa is a harmless snake, and the public must be educated not to kill it but to protect it. As the population and tourist industry of Jamaica grow, pressure on land – and the boa's habitat – will increase.

GOLDEN TOAD

Bufo periglenes
Family: BUFONIDAE
Order: ANURA

COSTA RICA

STATUS: Critically Endangered: (IUCN); CITES I. Probably none remain. Related endangered species: Amatola toad (*Bufo amatolicus*); boreal toad (*B. boreas*); Yosemite toad (*B. canorus*); black toad (*B. exsul*); Houston toad (*B. houstonensis*); Amargosa toad (*B. nelsoni*).

DISTRIBUTION: Montane (mountainous cloud forest) in Monteverde Cloud Forest Preserve, Cordillera de Tilaran, Costa Rica.

SIZE: Length: male 1.5–2in (4.1–4.8cm); female 1.8–2.3in (4.7–5.4cm).

FORM: Male red or orange; female is mottled black, red, or yellow.

DIET: Insects and other invertebrates.

BREEDING: Clutch size of about 300 eggs is laid March–June; eggs hatch into tadpoles.

CONSERVATION: The golden toad was first described in 1964 and in 1987 1,500 animals were counted, but in both 1988 and 1989 only one individual was recorded at Monteverde in Costa Rica. Since then not a single golden toad has been seen. Over the same period about 20 percent of the frog and toad species found at Monteverde declined dramatically in numbers. The species that were affected were those most dependent on standing water for breeding. The golden toad is one such species – it breeds in pools of rain that form around the roots of trees. The cause of this toad's dramatic population decline is not at all understood. Monteverde is a nature reserve and is not subject to habitat destruction of any kind, nor are any herbicides, pesticides, or other chemicals used in the region. It seems that climate change may be responsible for the demise of the golden toad. Since the 1970s the number of days has diminished when the cloud forest is actually shrouded in cloud, which has affected the local wildlife. It seems that the golden toads died out when their habitat became too dry for successful breeding.

DRYING AND DYING OUT
The golden toad is highly unusual in that the color of the male (below) is strikingly different from that of the female. The toad appears to have become a victim of climate change, dying out because its moist habitat has dried out.

HAMILTON'S FROG

Leiopelma hamiltoni
Family: LEIOPELMATIDAE
Order: ANURA

NEW ZEALAND

STATUS: Vulnerable (IUCN); not listed by CITES. Fewer than 200 remain. Related endangered species: Archey's frog (*Leiopelma archeyi*); Maud Island frog (*L. pakeka*).

DISTRIBUTION: Cool, humid areas in coastal forests of Stephens Island, New Zealand.

SIZE: Length: 1.5–2in (3.5–5cm).

FORM: Frog is light to dark brown with darker markings on the flanks; no tympanum (eardrum). The eyes have horizontal pupils; 9 vertebrae in the backbone (most frogs and toads have 8 or fewer). It swims by kicking its hind legs alternately.

DIET: Small invertebrates.

BREEDING: Eggs are laid on land; larval phase completed in the eggs, which hatch into tiny tailed froglets after about 5 weeks. Froglets climb onto the male's back, where they complete their development.

CONSERVATION: One of the world's rarest and most primitive frog species, the Hamilton's frog is confined to one island. Here it is found in an area of boulder-strewn ground no more than 656 square yards (600 sq m) in size. Isolated for centuries, New Zealand has become home to a unique endemic fauna (animals found only in one place), none of which are mammals. When mammals such as rats and pigs were introduced from other parts of the world, many native species were defenseless against these predators. Probably unable to coexist with introduced rodents, the Hamilton's frog retreated to remote habitats such as offshore islands.

In addition, much of the frogs' damp coastal forest habitat has been destroyed and replaced by farmland. The frog is threatened by further risks. First, a severe weather or pollution event could wipe them out. Second, in such a small population, there is the problem of inbreeding. The rescue plan for the frog involves continued habitat protection, plus the possibility of establishing additional populations elsewhere if suitable places can be found.

CONFINED FROG
Hamilton's frog is one of the rarest frog species in the world. It is confined to a single, tiny, protected locality in a cool, humid area of coastal forest in Stephens Island, New Zealand.

HARLEQUIN FROG

Atelopus various
Family: BUFONIDAE
Order: ANURA

COSTA
RICA

PANAMA

STATUS: Not listed by IUCN; not listed by CITES. Population unknown. Most of the 55 species of *Atelopus* are threatened endangered species.

DISTRIBUTION: Close to streams in wet and dry tropical forests in Costa Rica and Panama.

SIZE: Length: male 1–1.6in (2.5–4.1cm); female 1.3–2.3in (3.3–6cm).

FORM: Highly variable in color, it is usually yellow or red with black markings. The skin secretes powerful toxins, protecting it against predators. A pointed snout, slender body, and long limbs.

DIET: Small invertebrates.

BREEDING: Occurs during the wet season of May–December. The eggs are laid in pools October–December; the tadpoles hatch and develop quickly, metamorphosing before the pool dries out.

CONSERVATION: The brightly colored and highly aggressive harlequin frogs have a natural enemy that is unaffected by their toxins: a fly that lays its eggs on their skin. The eggs hatch into maggots that burrow into the frog, eventually killing it. It is possible that the fly is partly responsible for the recent decline that has occurred among the frogs. Periods of drought force frogs to congregate together in whatever damp places they can find, increasing the risk that parasitic flies, and other diseases, can get from one frog to another. Harlequin frogs were abundant until the late 1980s, but by 1992 they had disappeared from many areas.

That was a time of climate change, the result of which has been a general drying out of the habitat, with longer dry periods and fewer wet days. Another factor is that for the past 10 years, Central American frogs have suffered from a disease caused by a parasitic fungus that invades the skin of adults. The fungus may interfere with the passage of water and oxygen across a frog's skin, or produce a substance that is toxic to frogs.

DISEASE DANGERS
The harlequin frog's vivid coloration warns off most predators. However, that is no protection against an invasive fungus or the maggots that can burrow through the frog's skin.

199

AXOLOTL

Ambystoma mexicanum
Family: AMBYSTOMATIDAE
Order: CAUDATA

MEXICO

STATUS: Vulnerable (IUCN); CITES II. Unknown population. Related endangered species: California tiger salamander (*Ambystoma californiense*).

DISTRIBUTION: Lake Xochimilco, and nearby smaller lakes, in Mexico.

SIZE: Length: 4–8in (10–20cm).

FORM: A gray or black salamander; in captivity it is albino and other colors including yellow, and white with black or gray blotches. Large, wide head with rounded snout; plump body; large, laterally flattened tail; 3 pairs of feathery external gills behind head.

DIET: Small invertebrates.

BREEDING: In spring and fall the female lays up to 500 eggs, depositing them on the bottom of the lake. Axolotls remain as larvae throughout their life, retaining external gills and a tail.

CONSERVATION: For many years, the axolotl was collected for food and was sold in Mexico City as a delicacy. However, it has declined in the wild as the result of pollution and drainage of marshy areas around Lake Xochimilco, and it is now protected. Voracious predators, axolotls generally eat invertebrates such as worms and insect larvae, but will also readily eat their own kind. This is a well-known problem among axolotl breeders, who have to take precautions if they are to successfully rear young animals. Adult axolotls eat eggs and larvae, and larger larvae eat smaller ones. Cannibalistic larvae pay a price, however, in that they are more likely to pick up parasites and diseases than are those that feed

on invertebrate prey. Often smaller larvae that are attacked by other axolotls or by fish lose parts of their limbs, gills, or tail. There is a remarkable ability among salamanders of this type to regrow parts of their body that have been lost. This ability is a major reason why they are kept for scientific research. Understanding this ability to regrow parts of the body may help us better understand the healing of wounds and the transplanting of organs and limbs. For this reason, axolotls will continue to be bred in captivity.

LOSS OF LAKES
The main threat to the axolotl is loss and pollution of its habitat. The axolotl comes in a variety of color and albino forms in captivity, although in the wild it is black or gray.

JAPANESE GIANT SALAMANDER

Andrias japonicus
Family: CRYPTOBRANCHIDAE
Order: CAUDATA

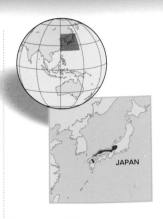

JAPAN

STATUS: Vulnerable (IUCN); CITES I. Unknown population. Related endangered species: Chinese giant salamander (*Andrias davidianus*).

DISTRIBUTION: Rocky mountain streams with clear, fast-flowing, and well-oxygenated water in southern Japanese islands of Honshu and Kyushu, at altitudes of 980–3,300ft (300–1000m).

SIZE: Length: 8–56in (20–140cm).

FORM: A large salamander with a long, flattened body and rough, warty skin with many wrinkles and folds. A laterally compressed tail with a dorsal (back) fin makes up a quarter of its total length. The broad, flat head has small eyes. The limbs are small and slightly flattened. It is reddish or grayish brown on upper body with a darker mottled pattern; paler below.

DIET: Fish, worms, and crustaceans such as crayfish.

BREEDING: Fall (August–September). The male digs a pit in gravel on a stream bed. The female lays 400–600 eggs in strings 7–60ft (2–18m) long, and the male sheds sperm onto them. After mating, the female leaves the male, who guards the eggs until they hatch, after about 2 months. The newly hatched larvae reach maturity at about 3 years and live up to 50 years or more.

CONSERVATION: The Japanese giant salamander and its relative the Chinese giant salamander are the world's largest salamanders. Its size, combined with its specific habitat needs, means that the Japanese giant salamander has

never been an abundant creature. It has been badly affected by deforestation in the mountainous areas of Honshu and Kyushu, the two Japanese islands where it lives. The damming of rivers in this region destroys the clear, well-oxygenated water that it needs for breeding and hunting, and thus is also causing a decline in numbers.

Giant salamanders have also been collected in the past and sent to many museums, aquaria, and zoos throughout the world. However, this kind of trade is now tightly controlled, the species having been given full protection under the CITES treaty.

HABITAT THREATS
The Japanese giant salamander's fast-flowing mountain stream habitat is under threat from damming and deforestation. It is, however, protected against any human trading for collectors.

OLM

Proteus anguinus
Family: PROTEIDAE
Order: CAUDATA

STATUS: Vulnerable (IUCN); not listed by CITES. Unknown numbers.

DISTRIBUTION: Caves and underground lakes and streams in limestone mountains of south-eastern Europe; the Adriatic coast from northern Italy to Montenegro.

SIZE: Length: 8–11in (20–28cm).

FORM: A large, flat head with a rounded snout; a white, pale-gray, pink, or creamy-yellow elongated body; darker blotches in the younger animals. It has large pink, feathery external gills and small rudimentary limbs.

HIDDEN THREATS
The olm is a bizarre, permanently aquatic salamander that lives almost entirely underground. It is vulnerable to a variety of factors that threaten its already restricted and specialized habitat.

DIET: Small aquatic invertebrates, mainly crustaceans.

BREEDING: Any time of year. The eggs are fertilized internally. Twelve to 70 eggs are laid under a stone and guarded by the female until hatched; alternatively, just 1–2 eggs develop inside the body of the female, who gives birth to well-developed larvae. Young mature at 7 years and the life span is up to 58 years.

CONSERVATION: The olm is a strange and obscure amphibian that is highly adapted to living in underground caves where there is water in the form of streams, pools, and lakes. The olm's specialized habitat requirements means that even under ideal conditions it will always be a rare species. Although it is reasonably safe from many of the changes, such as habitat destruction, that have adversely affected surface-living amphibians, it is not wholly unaffected by events on the surface. Much of the water that fills the underground caves flows in from the surface. It can then become contaminated by a range of pollutants, such as agricultural runoff or industrial waste. It is believed that pollution is a major factor in the reduction of the population of the olm.

Both scientists and amateur enthusiasts are fascinated by the olm. In the past olms were collected as pig food. Today the animals are collected by amphibian fanciers and this is having a more serious effect on natural populations.

GIANT CATFISH

Pangasianodon gigas
Family: PANGASIIDAE
Order: SILURIFORMES

STATUS: Endangered (IUCN); CITES I. Low population, but exact numbers unknown. Related endangered species: No close relatives, but Barnard's rock catfish (*Austroglanis barnardi*), in the same order of fish, is Critically Endangered.

DISTRIBUTION: Major watercourses and lakes of Mekong River system through Cambodia, Laos, Thailand, Vietnam, and (possibly) part of China.

SIZE: Length: 6.6–9.8ft (2–3m). Weight: 240–660lb (110–300kg).

FORM: The fish has an almost straight back profile, with a curved belly and a flattened head. Lower jaw barbels (whiskers) are absent. Large eyes are set low on head. Both dorsal and pectoral (chest) fins have spines along front edge; the tail fin is powerful and forked.

DIET: Vegetarian: algae and soft, succulent plants.

BREEDING: Migrates up to several thousand miles upriver between mid-April and end of May, possibly as far north as Lake Tali in Yunnan, China. Spawning in captive-bred specimens yields on average 17.6–22lb (8–10kg) of eggs.

CONSERVATION: Little is known about the life of the giant catfish, so it is difficult to say what influence environmental factors have had, or are having, on wild populations. However, it is known that intense fishing over many years brought the species to the brink of extinction. Not only does the giant catfish taste good, but the Thais believe that eating the fish leads to a long, healthy, and

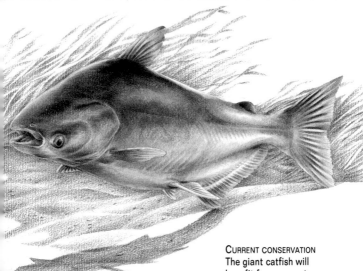

prosperous life. No wonder, then, that the giant catfish commands a high price in Thailand. The catfish has also been fished for its oil yield. The present situation may be more hopeful, since the release of 20,000 young catfish from captive-breeding programs into rivers previously inhabited by them. As more is learned about the catfish's biology and lifestyle, there will be a better understanding of how to conserve the species.

CURRENT CONSERVATION
The giant catfish will benefit from current research into its life-style. As conservation efforts – such as the release of captive-bred specimens and controlled fishing – take effect, the fortunes of the giant catfish could be about to take a turn for the better.

DWARF PYGMY GOBY

Pandaka pygmaea
Family: GOBIIDAE
Order: PERCIFORMES

STATUS: Critically Endangered (IUCN); not listed by CITES. Unknown population, but believed to be more than 80% lower than in the mid-1980s. Related endangered species: Nearly 60 species of goby are officially regarded as under some degree of threat, with 5 believed to be Critically Endangered, including Edgbaston goby (*Chlamydogobius squamigenus*).

DISTRIBUTION: Freshwater/ brackish (slightly salty) rivers and mangroves, usually close to shady banks in the Philippines and Indonesia; now reported from Bali, Singapore, and Sulawesi. Also reported to be found in genuinely marine conditions.

SIZE: Length: male up to 0.4in (1.1cm); female up to 0.6in (1.5cm).

FORM: Typical "goby" shape featuring a blunt, large head and a large eye. The fish's body tapers toward the caudal (tail) fin. The pelvic (hip) fins are fused into a powerful sucker. It has two dorsal (back) fins, and prominent black spots along the lower edge of posterior half of the body, between the anal (belly) fin and the base of the caudal fin.

DIET: Minute invertebrates.

BREEDING: Not many details are available, but known to include the protection of the eggs by at least 1 parent.

CONSERVATION: One of the main homes of the dwarf pygmy goby is mangrove swamps. Over the years, areas of this habitat have been drained, dredged, and polluted. The removal of trees and other plant cover poses one threat. Another is the construction of facilities for prawn farming. Some of the brackish areas where the dwarf pygmy goby lives have also been degraded. Fortunately because of its small size it is not fished. Nor is it popular with collectors because it is tiny. (So, both these activities do not pose threats to the ongoing survival of the species.) However, the combined effects of a decline in the size of the fish's range, along with a deterioration of its habitat, have resulted in population levels falling to 20 percent or less of the numbers recorded in the mid-1980s. As a result, the tiny dwarf pygmy goby is now listed by the IUCN as Critically Endangered.

THE WORLD'S SMALLEST KNOWN FISH
The dwarf pygmy goby's river and mangrove swamp habitat is now at risk from disturbances, including felling mangrove trees for charcoal.

RAZORBACK SUCKER

Xyrauchen texanus
Family: CATOSTOMIDAE
Order: CYPRINIFORMES

STATUS: Endangered (IUCN); not listed by CITES. U.S. Lake Mojave population probably fewer than 20,000. Green River population fewer than 500. Related endangered species: Harelip sucker (*Moxostoma lacerum*).

DISTRIBUTION: Warm, flowing waters; deep pools and eddies away from main channels of Lower Colorado River basin: Lakes Mojave, Mead, and Havasu. Upper Colorado basin: Green River, small numbers known in Lower Green River and Upper Colorado River in Grand Valley, and in San Juan and Colorado sections of Lake Powell.

SIZE: Length: 24in (60cm); can grow to about 39in (100cm). Weight: up to 10lb (4.5kg).

FORM: A pronounced keel starts behind the head and extends to the front edge of the dorsal (back) fin. Head is flattish; mouth underslung. Body is dark brownish black above, fading to white or yellow below.

USA

DAM DANGERS
The razorback sucker has suffered a dramatic decline due to human interventions such as dams and reservoirs, and the introduction of nonnative fish for sport. It is now in danger of extinction.

DIET: Algae, zooplankton, detritus, and aquatic invertebrates.

BREEDING: November–May (after upriver migration) in Lake Mojave. Mid-April–mid-May in Middle Green River, where water is cooler. Spawns near shore over pebbles or gravel. Mature at 4–7 years.

CONSERVATION: Threats to its survival include the large-mouth bass and the channel catfish, two species that have been introduced into its range to cater to the needs of sport anglers. These two have wiped out large populations of razorback in lakes and reservoirs. Introduced fish used for bait also prey on the razorbacks' fry (young). The razorback freely mates with the flannelmouth sucker. This leads to hybrid fish and is so frequent in parts of the razorback's range, that affected populations may become extinct. Alterations to its U.S. habitat are another factor. Dams, and the reservoirs they create, form major barriers to spawning migrations. Other water-management projects (and pollution) have also affected the razorback. A protection project is underway that includes restoring watercourse flows, restocking, and control of "sport" species.

VALENCIA TOOTHCARP

Valencia hispanica
Family: VALENCIIDAE
Order: CYPRINODONTIFORMES

SPAIN

STATUS: Endangered (IUCN); not listed by CITES. Numbers unknown, but restricted to just 3 populations. Related endangered species: Corfu toothcarp (*Valencia letourneuxi*).

DISTRIBUTION: Clean, clear, slow-flowing or standing waters with dense aquatic vegetation in 3 locations in Spain: two near Valencia and one near Castellón.

SIZE: Female up to 2.8in (7cm); male smaller.

FORM: An elongated, laterally compressed body, with large eyes, well-formed, rounded fins. Males at Castellón site are uniform bluish-green; those from other localities have brown sheen in anterior half of the body. All carry thin, vertical stripes, particularly in posterior half of body. Female drabber (browner).

DIET: Small aquatic invertebrates; small flying insects that may fall into the water.

BREEDING: Two peaks of activity in spawning season: early spring and the end of summer. The males establish territories that are visited by the females. The eggs are laid among fine-leaved vegetation; hatching takes about 1 week.

CONSERVATION: The natural habitat of the Valencia toothcarp is clean, clear, slow-flowing or static, well-vegetated bodies of water. The tourist industry has become a major threat to the fish's habitats. The construction of holiday resorts, for example, has led to the destruction of its habitat and increased water pollution. Water channeling for irrigation or water supply is another threat.

Introduced species, such as the mosquitofish, have also put the fish under severe pressure. The rescue plan for the Valencia toothcarp includes a captive-breeding program. However, it is essential that some of the fish's existing locations are protected, so that the habitat recovers sufficiently to allow the Valencia fishcarp populations to expand.

VERTEBRATE ON THE VERGE
The valencia fishcarp is rated as one of the world's 24 most endangered species of vertebrate. The mosquitofish – introduced in the 1920s – competes with the Valencia for space and for food, including mosquitoes.

ATLANTIC COD

Gadus morhua
Family: GADIDAE
Order: GADIFORMES

STATUS: Vulnerable (IUCN); not listed by CITES. Numbers are low enough to be endangered or vulnerable. Related endangered species: Haddock (*Melanogrammus aeglefinus*).

DISTRIBUTION: North Atlantic, where juveniles live just below the lower tidal zone to about 66ft (20m); adults found from 66ft (20m) down to 260ft (80m).

SIZE: Length: 30–70in (80–180cm). Weight: 80–211lb (36–96kg).

FORM: A stout but streamlined fish. Well-developed barbel (whisker) on chin, 3 dorsal (back) and 2 anal (belly) fins. Coloration varies: may be olive-brown on the back, shading into lighter tones toward the whitish belly. The base color is overlaid with dark spots.

DIET: A bottom-feeder with a strong preference for mollusks, crustacea, worms, and smaller fish.

BREEDING: Spawns February–April/May at about 660ft (200m). In some areas spawning may take place at 66–330ft (20–100m). Up to 9 million eggs are released by a large female. Eggs and larvae are left to fend for themselves.

CONSERVATION: In the 19th century, some cod weighing up to 200lbs (90kg) were recorded. Now, after years of intensive fishing, even a cod of 40lb (18kg) is considered large. Up until the 1950s, annual catches of 400 million cod seemed not to affect population levels. Then came factory trawlers with gigantic nets. During the mid-1950s and 1960s catches rose dramatically. Then they dropped just as fast. In the late 1970s the new "dragger" trawlers arrived. Their nets trapped huge numbers of fish, but also plowed up the bottom, destroying the habitats on which the cod depended for their survival. Heavy losses caused by fast-expanding seal populations may also have led to their decline. In 1992 a ban was imposed on cod fishing around Newfoundland, with further restrictions following in other cod-fishing areas. In 2001 the European Union ordered an emergency ban on all deep-sea fishing in the Atlantic between Britain and Northern Europe to prevent the collapse of cod stocks.

OVERFISHED
The Atlantic cod may cease to be a food on the tables of Europe and North America, as modern fishing trawlers have depleted stocks of this once-abundant fish.

GREAT WHITE SHARK

Carcharodon carcharias
Family: LAMNIDAE
Order: LAMNIFORMES

STATUS: Vulnerable (IUCN); not listed by CITES. About 10,000 remain. The whale shark (*Rhincodon typus*) is a related endangered species.

DISTRIBUTION: Wide range of habitats worldwide, but mostly in warm-temperature and subtropical waters; may also be found in warmer areas. Found between the surface and depths of 820ft (250m) or more from surf line to offshore (rarely in mid-ocean). Only infrequently encountered in colder northern regions.

SIZE: Confirmed data indicate a maximum size of 18–20ft (5.5–6m).

FORM: A torpedo-shaped fish with saw-edged triangular teeth. Has a system of sensory organs for detecting prey; and a light-sensitive membrane below retina for tracking movement in dim light.

DIET: Mainly bony fish but also cartilaginous fish (including other sharks); marine mammals, including cetaceans (whales and dolphins) and pinnipeds (seals and sea lions).

BREEDING: Gives birth to 5–10 live young (probably more) after a gestation period that could last as long as 1 year.

CONSERVATION: Over the years, great white shark numbers have declined as they have been killed for sport by professional anglers or to obtain shark products for the souvenir trade. The sharks have also been caught in nets set out for other target species, while shark nets installed to protect bathers along beaches have also taken their toll. The actual extent of decline and the total number of great whites that remain in the wild are difficult to quantify for reasons that include the different roaming habits of different fish. Indeed worldwide, the species is still relatively scarce.

As a result, the figure of 10,000 specimens remaining can only be approximate. Concerned by the decline, several countries have started protection programs. Measures range from banning all great white shark products to forbidding fishing and underwater viewing by tourists. Further action is being urged by conservation bodies who fear that the current IUCN listing as Vulnerable many be incorrect and that the great white shark may already be Endangered.

HUNTING THE HUNTER
The great white shark is a fierce sea predator with a finely tuned sensory system.

WHALE SHARK

Rhincodon typus
Family: RHINCODONTIDAE
Order: ORECTOLOBIFORMES

STATUS: Vulnerable (IUCN); not listed by CITES. Unknown population. Many related endangered species including basking shark (*Cetorhinus maximus*); great white shark (*Carcharodon carcharias*).

DISTRIBUTION: Tropical and temperate areas of Atlantic, Indian, and Pacific Oceans, both inshore and deep sea.

SIZE: Length: 39ft (12m); may grow to 59ft (18m).

FORM: A whalelike shark with a broad, flat head, truncated snout, and large mouth with small teeth. Grayish in color, with individual patterns of light spots and stripes.

DIET: Zooplankton, small fish, and other small animals.

BREEDING: Internal fertilization; the fertilized eggs hatch within female's body; the young measure 16–20in (40–50cm) at birth.

CONSERVATION: The whale sharks' habit of forming large groups in certain areas of the ocean means that they have been seen by many people including tourists, divers, conservationists, and scientists. This has raised people's awareness of their vulnerability and the threat to their survival. However, whale sharks do have human predators, and local hunting has taken a severe toll on their populations. In one year alone, it is reported that as many as 1,000 whales were killed by fishermen from just three Indian villages.

No one knows whether there are separate populations of whale sharks or just one single, migratory population. If there is only one population, then 1,000 losses a year will be extremely harmful to the species. There are numerous

aspects of their biology that are not yet fully understood despite better research.

Ironically, a lack of knowledge is a reason why the whale shark has not been exploited commercially. Action is being taken by several countries to gather information about the creature, and measures are being implemented to protect existing fish. Conservation programs have been set up on the eastern seaboard of the U.S., the Maldives, the Philippines, and Western Australia. It is hoped that data from the projects can be used to help ensure the whales' survival. Extending the projects to other parts of their range will help, too.

THE WORLD'S LARGEST LIVING FISH
The whale shark is a placid creature, and divers can approach one safely. Because they are harmless, whale sharks have had a lot of contact with humans. This has contributed to their decline; they have become easy prey for fishermen.

COELACANTH

Latimeria chalumnae
Family: LATIMERIIDAE
Order: COELOCANTHIFORMES

Comoro Islands

MADAGASCAR

STATUS: Critically Endangered (IUCN); CITES I. Unknown population, but estimated at 200–500. Related endangered species: Sulawesi coelacanth (*Latimeria menadoensis*).

DISTRIBUTION: Cold waters in deep ocean at 240ft (70m) off Comoro Islands, Indian Ocean (between Madagascar and southeastern Africa).

SIZE: Length: up to 5.9ft (1.8m). Weight 210lb (95kg).

FORM: A primitive fish with limblike pectoral fins. A bluish base color has pinkish-white patches.

DIET: Fish.

BREEDING: Produces up to 20 large eggs, each measuring 3.5in (9cm) in diameter and weighing 10.6–12.4oz (300–350g). These are released within its body and the developing embryos reach a length of at least 12in (30cm) before the female gives birth. Life span is at least 11 years.

CONSERVATION: Rediscovered in 1938 by fishermen off the coast of South Africa, the coelacanth had been thought to be extinct for 70 million years. Since then, other catches have been recorded. However, specimens found near the Indonesian Island of Sulawesi have turned out to belong to a separate species identical in every way except coloration (they are brown with golden-colored flecks). Although it is impossible to gauge how abundant coelacanths are, there is no doubt that they are very rare and their re-discovery very exciting for conservationists.
In recognition of its rarity CITES has listed the coelacanth under

Appendix I, thus making trade in the fish illegal. Another protective measure involves the safe release of any specimens accidentally caught by fishermen. The coelacanth favors cold waters at depths of about 240ft (70m).
A "deep release kit" allows the fish to be lowered rapidly in a sack to a depth where the water is cold enough and where the fish can release itself safely. So far the method has proved to be the most effective way of returning coelacanths to the wild.

LIVING FOSSILS
Coelacanths, of which fewer than 500 are believed to exist, are pre-historic deep-sea bony fish. They are closely related to the ancestors of land vertebrates and so-called living fossils.

SWAN GALAXIAS

Galaxias fontanus
Family: GALAXIIDAE
Order: OSMERIFORMES

AUSTRALIA

Tasmania

STATUS: Critically Endangered (IUCN); not listed by CITES. Population is unknown; once near extinction, but now expanding. Related endangered species: Barred galaxias (*galaxias fuscus*); clarence galaxias (*G. johnstoni*); pedder galaxias (*G. pedderensis*).

DISTRIBUTION: Cool, flowing waters of Tasmania; primarily pools and shallow-water stretches of stream edges in, at most, several headwater streams of the Swan and Macquarie Rivers in eastern Tasmania; several populations from translocated stocks now established.

SIZE: Length: up to maximum of 5.3in (13.5cm).

FORM: A tubular body; dorsal (back) and anal (belly) fins are set well back; no second dorsal fin. The head is flattened with large eyes and a blunt snout. A brown to olive-colored body with irregular mottling and a light-colored belly.

DIET: Aquatic and terrestrial insects; some aquatic invertebrates and algae.

BREEDING: No spawning migrations occur. Spawning is restricted to the spring months, but exact spawning sites, or their nature, are unknown.

CONSERVATION: In 1862 the European perch was introduced into Tasmania, followed, two years later, by the arrival in Australia of the brown trout. Together the two predators decimated the local Swan galaxias population, which presented an easy target because of its tendency to gather in open-water pools.

INTRODUCED PROBLEMS
The swan galaxias lives its whole life in fresh water. The populations are thought to be expanding, however, Swan galaxias are still at risk from predation by introduced species.

The result, over more than 100 years, has been a progressive reduction in its numbers and range. It is likely that the galaxias' continued presence is the result of natural barriers such as waterfalls, which prevent the brown trout and perch from gaining access to these stretches of water. In 1989 a relocation program was initiated that transferred stocks to places out of the reach of predators, and the results have been encouraging. However, if any predatory exotic species are released into the galaxias' strongholds, it would spell disaster.

MASKED ANGELFISH

Genicanthus personatus
Family: POMACANTHIDAE
Order: PERCIFORMES

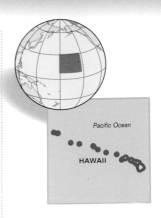

Pacific Ocean

HAWAII

STATUS: Lowest Risk (IUCN); not listed by CITES. Unknown population. Related endangered species: Resplendent pygmy angelfish (*Centropyge resplendens*).

DISTRIBUTION: Northwestern islands of the Hawaiian chain at depths of about 60ft (18m) downward. (A depth of 275ft (84m) has been recorded for 1 specimen.) Often found in open water close to reef drop-offs.

SIZE: Up to 10in (25cm) reported for male; perhaps slightly smaller for female.

FORM: The male is grayish-white with a yellow or yellow-gold "face mask" and fins. The tail fin has a white edge with vertical black band in front half. The top and bottom rays are extended into filaments. The female has an ivory white body and fins. "Face mask" is black. It lacks fin extensions, but it has the vertical black band.

DIET: Mainly zooplankton (minute animal life).

BREEDING: No details available, although it is known that the female can change sex over a period of 2 to 3 weeks, if the dominant male of a group is no longer present.

CONSERVATION: The rare and exceptionally beautiful masked angelfish has never been observed in large numbers. It is not known if it is more abundant at depths below 260ft (75m) – beyond the reach of scuba divers. It might be that specimens occasionally collected by divers are only those that live at the shallow edge of the reef.

If so, the masked angelfish may be more abundant than we currently believe it to be. Even if this were the case, captive breeding may still serve as an important "insurance policy" for the future of the species. It would be a means of providing stocks not just for aquaria but for restocking of natural habitats should this ever become necessary. At present, captive breeding still presents a considerable challenge.

LITTLE KNOWN FISH
Greater knowledge of the fish's lifestyle is needed before it can be bred in captivity. What is obvious is the male's golden "mask" and fins. The female's coloration is very different.

MOJARRA CARACOLERA

Nandopsis bartoni
Family: CICHLIDAE
Order: PERCIFORMES

MEXICO

STATUS: Vulnerable (IUCN); not listed by CITES. Population about 10,000. Related endangered species include mojarra caracolera de Cuatro Ciénegas (*Herichthys* or *Cichlasoma minckleyi*) and mojarra de Bulha (*Nandopsis urophthalmus ericymba*).

DISTRIBUTION: Springs, streams, and lagoons mostly with clear water, including Laguna Media Luna in Rio Verde Valley, San Luis de Potosí, Mexico. Vegetation, including water lilies; the substratum (bottom) is often covered with detritus.

SIZE: Length: about 7in (18cm).

FORM: The body of this fish is compressed; males develop a hump on the head as they mature. In both sexes the lower half of the body becomes black at breeding time; the top half is white or gray-blue. At other times their bodies have a pattern of irregular vertical dark bands.

DIET: Encrusting algae; will also take aquatic invertebrates.

BREEDING: Lays eggs in caves or close to a rock. Several hundred adhesive eggs are laid and guarded by the female; the male will defend the territory. Hatching occurs after 2 days; both parents protect the fry (baby fish) during the first few days, until they become free-swimming and disperse.

CONSERVATION: The colorful mojarra is threatened by the introduction of a number of exotic (nonnative) species to the region. As well as competing for space, the nonnative species compete with the mojarras for food.

In addition, predation on their eggs
and young are taking their toll.
Over the past decade or so the
decline has been estimated at
about 20 percent with a further
similar drop expected in the future.
Fortunately, the species is bred in
considerable numbers commercially
throughout the world, to cater to
aquarium keepers.

**NONNATIVE
COMPETITION**
Mojarra caracoleras
are under threat
from introduced
species in their
native Mexican
freshwaters.

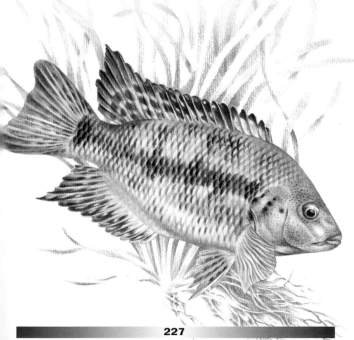

TOTOABA

Totoaba macdonaldi
Family: SCIAENIDAE
Order: PERCIFORMES

STATUS: Critically Endangered (IUCN); CITES I. Population unknown.

DISTRIBUTION: Deep waters of the Gulf of California, Mexico; shallow estuarine or marshy (brackish) waters in spawning season.

SIZE: Length: up to 6.6ft (2m). Weight: up to 300lb (135kg).

FORM: A perchlike fish; dull-colored on top, fading to lighter tones below. It has 2 dorsal (back) fins (1 with a deep notch); the back edge of the first just touches the front edge of the second; large head and mouth; lateral line organ (pressure-sensitive organ) on the side from the head back into tail.

DIET: Fish, shrimp, and other crustacea.

BREEDING: Migrates in spring to shallow estuarine or marshy brackish areas in the delta of Rio Colorado for spawning.

After spawning, the adults migrate south into deeper water. The juveniles are thought to stay in the northern Gulf for about 2 years.

CONSERVATION: The totoaba was once numerous; however, during the 1920s it began to be fished for its swim bladder – the organ that allows fish to control their buoyancy, letting the fish float or sink. Swim bladders were exported to Southeast Asia, where they are a delicacy, to be cooked and eaten or used as stock for soup. Catches declined and the industry collapsed chiefly because of the large numbers of fish being collected, Large numbers of juveniles were being caught by shrimp trawlers.

Fishing during the breeding season was banned and a sanctuary created. However, damming of the Colorado River caused shrinking of the fish's marshy spawning ground and a reduction in freshwater flow. By 1979, the totoaba was declared an endangered species. The establishment of a biosphere reserve in the Upper Gulf in 1993 has been beneficial, and captive breeding may also help protect the species.

RIVER MANAGEMENT
The Colorado River will need effective management if the totoaba is to avoid extinction in the near future. The totoaba faces continued threats from illegal fishing and changes to its water flow.

TROUT COD

Maccullochella macquariensis
Family: PERCICHTHYIDAE
Order: PERCIFORMES

AUSTRALIA

STATUS: Endangered (IUCN); not listed by CITES. Numbers unknown. Related endangered species: Clarence River cod (*Maccullochella ikei*); Mary River cod (*M. peelii mariensis*); Oxleyan pygmy perch (*Nannoperca oxleyana*).

DISTRIBUTION: A section of the Murray River and Seven Creeks in Victoria, Australia, where juveniles shelter under boulders and other cover in fast-flowing stretches; adults prefer deep pools.

SIZE: Length: 16–20in (40–50cm). Weight: 3.3–6.6lb (1.5–3kg).

FORM: A streamlined body. Blue-gray to brown on top, paler below; overlaid by spots and streaks. Fins dusky with white, yellow, or orange edges. Head has deep, gray-black stripe running from tip of the snout, through eye, to edge of gill cover.

DIET: Insects, tadpoles, crustaceans, and fish.

BREEDING: Pair bonding is believed to exist. Spawning is thought to be annual, usually in spring or summer. Adhesive eggs laid on logs or rocks; eggs hatch after 5–10 days. Newly hatched fry begin feeding some 10 days later. Fully mature at 3–5 years.

CONSERVATION: The trout cod has suffered from overfishing and alteration to its habitat. Formerly shaded and forested areas have been exposed to the sun. As a result, water temperatures have risen, sediment has increased, and the water quality has deteriorated. Potentially more dangerous are the effects of introduced species of "exotic" fish.

ONCE ABUNDANT
The trout cod was once abundant and widespread in several rivers in southeastern Australia. Today, only two self-sustaining populations are left, but a rescue program is in place.

Such introductions bring new disease organisms. As yet, there is no conclusive evidence that the trout cod is affected, but there is cause for concern. Measures being taken to preserve the species range from researching the fish's biology and ecology, to captive breeding for restocking, angling bans, education, and legislation. Hatchery-bred fish are already being used to restock trout cod habitats. Monitoring will show whether or not, in the future, the released specimens are breeding in the wild.

WATERCRESS DARTER

Etheostoma nuchale
Family: PERCIDAE
Order: PERCIFORMES

STATUS: Endangered (IUCN); not listed by CITES. No current population figures available; 22 other species of *Etheostoma* are listed by IUCN as related endangered species.

DISTRIBUTION: Heavily vegetated pools and runs in 3 springs in Jefferson County, Alabama (Glenn Springs, Thomas's Spring, and Roebuck Springs) in which the dominant plants include watercress and algae.

SIZE: About 2.1in (5.4cm), but up to 2.5in (6.4cm) reported.

FORM: A slightly compressed body with 2 dorsal (back) fins. The males have bright orange-red bellies and blue and orange fins during the breeding season; the females are less brightly colored.

DIET: Mainly small aquatic snails, crustaceans, and insects.

BREEDING: Probably March–July.

CONSERVATION: The watercress darter was discovered in 1964 at Glenn Springs, Alabama – a small site only 60ft (18m) from a busy highway. The species was immediately identified as at risk from chemical spillage plus the effects on the water supply of nearby shopping complexes and apartments. The Watercress Darter Recovery Team was set up to search for other populations. Two other sites at springs were identified, one of which had dangerously high levels of water contamination. Thomas's Spring tested clean and seemed to be a good habitat for the darter – until the grass carp was introduced to clear the pool of vegetation. The grass carp deprived the watercress darter of essential cover and its diet of aquatic invertebrates. In 1980, the grass carp were removed, the spring became revegetated, and the watercress darter began to reestablish itself. The high levels of pollution at the other two springs is causing the darter populations there to decline. Small populations have been introduced into suitable "transplant" sites, some of which have disappeared, while others are reported to be doing well.

WATERCRESS DEPENDENT
The watercress darter inhabits just three springs, where it is dependent upon watercress plants for survival. Some fish have been moved to other springs with limited success – their position is still precarious.

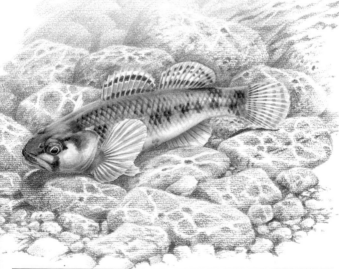

AVALON HAIRSTREAK BUTTERFLY

Strymon avalona
Family: LYCAENIDAE
Order: LEPIDOPTERA

STATUS: Vulnerable (IUCN); not listed by CITES. Unknown population but 3 other hairstreak butterflies in the U.S. may face similar threats.

DISTRIBUTION: Chaparral (dense area of shrubs, brushwood, and trees, especially oaks) and grass in Santa Catalina Island, California.

SIZE: Wingspan: 0.7in (1.9–2.5cm).

FORM: A typical butterfly. Two pairs of wings; each hind wing bears 1 short, thin taillike extension. Upper side of the wings grayish; the upper sides of hind wings bear yellow or red spot near the tail and may have small, whitish spots near the edge. A fine, light row of dots or hairline markings on the undersides of both wing pairs.

DIET: Caterpillars feed on silverleaf lotus and deerbrush lotus. Adults feed on nectar from common summac and giant buckwheat or St. Catherine's lace.

BREEDING: The female usually lays 1 batch per year of round, flat eggs, looking like minute cookies, and geometrically patterned. The eggs are laid on the ends of the stems and on the flower buds of silverleaf lotus, island broom, or deerbrush lotus. Sluglike caterpillars (larvae) emerge from February to December. The caterpillars feed on the flowers and leaves of trees and bushes rather than on herbaceous plants.

CONSERVATION: The Avalon hairstreak butterfly is one of the rarest and most isolated butterfly species in the United States. It is named for the town of Avalon on Santa Catalina Island, to which it is endemic, which means that it is found nowhere else. The isolated position of the island has allowed the butterfly to survive. It has had no predators or competition by species with similar requirements. Such pressures may have led to the butterfly's extinction on the mainland. It is possible, however, that the butterfly may have evolved only on Santa Catalina Island.

The need for conservation of the Avalon hairstreak's habitat and host plants is appreciated by the authorities, who have done much to publicize the vulnerability of this rare butterfly.

TAIL SAFE
The Avalon hairstreak has a short "tail" on each hind wing. When the insect settles, the tails are often made to quiver or tremble, and it is thought that some predators mistake them for antennae. The predator may then attack the wrong end of the butterfly, which is less likely to prove fatal.

HERMES COPPER BUTTERFLY

Lycaena hermes
Family: LYCAENIDAE
Order: LEPIDOPTERA

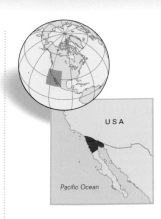

STATUS: Vulnerable (IUCN); not listed by CITES. Unknown population. Related endangered species: Avalon hairstreak butterfly (Strymon avalona).

DISTRIBUTION: Mixed woodlands, chaparral (dense growth of shrubs and trees) and coastal shrub in California; range restricted to San Diego County and Baja California.

SIZE: Wingspan: 1–1.3in (2.5–3.2cm).

FORM: 2 pairs of conspicuous wings; each hind wing bears 1 short "tail". Upper side brown with yellow-orange patch surrounding black spots; underside bright yellow; forewing with 4–6 black spots; hind wing with 3–6 black spots. Caterpillars (larva) are apple to dark green and have much simpler eyes than adult butterflies.

DIET: Caterpillars feed on redberry. Adults feed on nectar from flowers of wild buckwheat.

BREEDING: The male settles on a plant to watch for females. Single eggs are laid on the twigs of the redberry, the caterpillar host plant; the pupae hatch from end of May to mid-June. After hatching, the young caterpillars feed on the new young shoots of the host plant.

CONSERVATION: Increasing urban growth is causing problems for wildlife in California and other rapidly developing parts of the United States – including the Hermes copper butterfly. Industrial building sites, new roads, and electricity lines cause the break up of habitats into smaller and smaller sectors, and breeding groups become isolated from one another.

Butterflies are also becoming restricted to bits of habitat that are not big enough to support them. This reduces the breeding strength of the population.

Another problem for butterflies is forest fires, which put the insects, and their food, at risk. The use of pesticides and herbicides is also damaging to adult butterflies, their caterpillars, and their food plants. The Hermes copper is listed as rare or local throughout its range, and a strategy is needed to protect it from further habitat loss. Greater public awareness, particularly among local government officers and the construction industry, would help its future.

URBAN ENCROACHMENT
The hermes copper butterfly has a distribution limited to the district around San Diego and the northern end of Baja California. Its habitat is being damaged both by urban developers and by forest fires.

BLUE GROUND BEETLE

Carabus intricatus
Family: CARABIDAE
Order: COLEOPTERA

STATUS: Lower Risk (IUCN); not listed by CITES. Unknown population. Related endangered species: *Carabus olympiae* (no common name); delta green ground beetle (*Elaphrus viridis*).

DISTRIBUTION: Temperate woodland dominated by oak and beech trees in northwestern and central Europe.

SIZE: Length: adult 0.9–1.4in (2.4–3.6cm).

FORM: A slender beetle with oval, flattened body, usually metallic blue, but other color variants exist. Outer surfaces of the wing cases have a particular pattern that identifies the blue ground beetle from other beetle species. Well-developed eyes and antennae.

DIET: Insects, such as cockchafer larvae; worms, slugs, and snails.

BREEDING: Mating takes place in the fall before winter hibernation.

Long, slender larvae develop from eggs and feed actively before hiding underground in burrows where they pupate, emerging as adult beetles.

CONSERVATION: The attractive blue ground beetle has been recorded across much of Europe, from the Mediterranean in the south to Scandinavia in the north, and from Britain in the west to Poland in the east. However, despite its wide overall distribution, it is rare and in decline in most countries, since it is found in only a few localities. It is Britain's largest species of ground beetle and has been recorded there from five sites. However, a recent survey found positive evidence of the species at only two sites.

The blue ground beetle's preferred habitats are mature woodlands dominated by beech and oak trees where there is little ground vegetation. They like the high humidity provided by the layer

RESTRICTED HABITAT
The blue ground beetle is restricted to oak and beech woodlands where there is little undergrowth. Changes in woodland management have caused its decline.

of soil made of rotting leaves and bark. Their narrow range and need for particular environmental conditions means that they are vulnerable to the habitat changes that are the main threat to blue ground beetles today. The dense vegetation on the woodland floor is disrupted by changes in grazing patterns or the breaking up of the woodland canopy, which keeps out much of the light. The replacement of deciduous trees by coniferous trees is another threat to the habitat. Restoration programs in several European countries include allowing laboratory-raised beetles to be reintroduced into the wild.

EDIBLE SEA-URCHIN

Echinus esculentus
Family: ECHINIDAE
Order: ECHINIDA

STATUS: Lower Risk (IUCN); not listed by CITES. Unknown population. Probably several related endangered species including the rock borer *Paracentrotus lividus* (no common name). The species has been seriously overfished for its edible roe in parts of France and Ireland.

DISTRIBUTION: Rocks and seaweeds from the low tide mark down to 164ft (50m) in the northeastern Atlantic.

SIZE: Up to 6.7in (17cm) diameter; often smaller.

FORM: A large, globular body with a pale, rosy-pink test (shell-like internal skeleton) of chalky plates bearing whitish-pink, needle-shaped, movable spines with purple tips. Extendible, long, branched tentacles (called tube-feet) end in suckers. It has no head and no true brain. Mouth is on the underside of the test with complex arrangement of five jaws with teeth.

DIET: Barnacles, and large algae (plants without true stems, roots, and leaves).

BREEDING: Seasonal spawning; fertilization occurs in the open water; free-swimming larva feeds on minute drifting plants until it metamorphoses to form a juvenile urchin.

CONSERVATION: The beautifully colored edible sea-urchin was for centuries fished for its roe (eggs); the food was considered a delicacy in the 15th and 16th centuries. Unlike the smaller Mediterranean species *Paracentrotus lividus*, which has a more delicate roe, the coarse roe of the edible sea-urchin is no longer considered desirable to eat. The edible sea-urchin is easily collected, and the test (shell) cleaned out by removing the intestine and reproductive organs. The test then makes an attractive ornament – a familiar sight in beach souvenir shops.

In recent decades divers have collected edible sea-urchins from southwestern Britain in such large numbers that scientists now believe that a population crash may be imminent. However, further information is needed about the state of the populations of edible sea-urchins around northwestern Europe, and their life span, so that measures can be taken to protect them. They play a vital part in marine life, as they graze on algae; a lack of sea-urchins can result in rapid algae growth.

SHELL SEEKERS
The edible sea-urchin is collected extensively because its test (shell-like internal skeloton) makes it a popular decorative object or souvenir. The test is so close to the outside of the animal it seems like a shell; but it is covered in living tissue.

GIANT CLAM

Tridacna gigas
Family: TRIDACNIDAE
Order: VENEROIDA

STATUS: Vulnerable (IUCN); CITES II. Unknown population. Probably many related endangered species including red coral (*Corallium rubrum*), which is exploited in the Mediterranean.

DISTRIBUTION: Attached to rocks and reef-building corals in shallow water of tropical seas in Asia-Pacific regions.

SIZE: May reach 41in (104cm). Weight: up to 500lb (227kg).

FORM: A typical bivalve shell shape with massive, slow-growing, thick, scalloped valves (shells) hinged to protect soft body; bright and often vividly colored flesh visible when shells gape. Inhaling syphon and gills covered with cells bearing cilia (fine threadlike extensions) for taking in food.

DIET: Minute drifting planktonic organisms and the products of photosynthesis by microscopic plants living on the clam's body.

BREEDING: Each clam has male and female sex organs; a free-swimming larva results from the external fertilization of eggs. The larva attaches itself to a new substrate and develops into a new colony, which produces new zooids (independent animal bodies).

CONSERVATION: The massive and beautiful giant clams are virtually immobile, so they are easy game for souvenir hunters. Their shells have been used in native societies as house decorations and even as baptismal fonts. They have also been exploited since the 1960s to supply the Taiwanese market's demand for giant clam adductor muscle for human consumption.
   In 1983 the IUCN identified severe depletion of the species, particularly in the coral reefs of Indonesia, the Philippines, Papua New Guinea, and the islands of Micronesia, as well as of southern Japan.

Fortunately, techniques for cultivating the giant clam were developed during the late 1980s. They are now cultivated in hatcheries in the Asia-Pacific region and used to restock depleted reefs.

HATCHERY RESTOCKING
The giant clam has thick shells with corrugated edges. Easily collected by souvenir hunters, giant clams are rare; however hatchery-bred specimens are now being used to restock the reefs.

Hermit Beetle

Osmoderma eremita
Family: Scarabaeidae
Order: Coleoptera

Status: Vulnerable (IUCN); not listed by CITES. Unknown population. Related endangered species: Ciervo scarab beetle (*Aegialia concinna*); Guiliana's dune scarab beetle (*Pseudocotalpa guiliana*).

Distribution: Decaying trees: oaks and limes in western, central, and northern Europe.

Size: Length: 1.4in (3.6cm), excluding antennae.

Form: A beetle with a dark-colored body shaped like a narrow shield, short legs with flattened middle joints, and short antennae.

Diet: Decaying timber in mature woods; dung balls stored in a hole.

Breeding: Eggs laid in timber develop into grubs (larvae), which metamorphose into adult beetles. Eggs also laid in dung balls. Larvae feed inside, keeping outer crust intact before emerging as adults.

Conservation: Related to the dung beetle, the hermit beetle is a timber-loving species that is associated with decaying trees (they particularly like hollow trees). Host trees are usually common oaks or small-leaved lime trees, which are widely distributed across western, central, and northern Europe. Recent research using radio transmitters suggests that the beetle populations are more or less self-contained, and there is not much exchange of individuals from one tree to the next; for some reason the beetles do not seem to disperse very freely. Consequently, several generations may live continuously in the same tree. This makes them particularly vulnerable if the trees are cut down or the habitat altered in some way. Areas where oak and lime trees have existed for years are the most likely habitats for hermit beetles, but these trees are becoming increasingly scarce. The hermit beetle is now believed to be

endangered right across its European distribution. However, the hermit beetle appears to be secure in southern Sweden, where it is being extensively studied. A recent report has brought a new threat to light: the beetles are now being openly traded by collectors using the Internet and other media. This represents a further danger to the stability of the natural populations of the hermit beetles.

ATTACHED TO TREES
Hermit beetles live all their lives in decaying oak and lime trees. Since the beetles do not disperse well, isolated populations build up in each tree. If the tree dies, the beetles may be lost.

RED-KNEED TARANTULA

Euathlus smithi
Family: THERAPHOSIDAE
Order: ARANEAE

STATUS: Lower Risk (IUCN); not listed by CITES. Unknown population.

DISTRIBUTION: Scrubland and desert of northern Mexico and southern U.S. with temperatures of 70–90°F (20–30°C) and humidity of 60 percent.

SIZE: Length: up to 2.5in (6.4cm); leg span: up to 5in (12.7cm).

FORM: A cephalothorax (an arachnid with a joined head and thorax). The red-kneed tarantula's abdomen has 4 pairs of strikingly patterned legs tipped with gripping claws. Eight eyes on the head allow all-round (but poor) vision.
  Males have a thin body and long legs; mature males have tibial spurs (sharp projections) on pedipalps (appendages near the mouth) to grip female's fangs during mating.

DIET: Insects; also small animals such as lizards and mice.

BREEDING: Female produces eggs wrapped in silk. Spiderlings are guarded for several weeks after hatching. Life span of the males is 7–8 years; females 20–25 years in captivity.

CONSERVATION: The red-kneed tarantula is arguably the most popular of all pet tarantulas, and people have been collecting specimens since the 1970s. First discovered in 1888, the spider was soon recognized as having potential as a pet. It was also used to scare people in movies such as *Raiders of the Lost Ark*. Such publicity encouraged collection, and high sales in pet stores for many years. However, although they are easy to

keep, they are not easy to breed in captivity as their reproductive rate tends to be slow. Yet the spider's popularity continues to spur black-market smuggling across Mexico. As a result wild red-kneed tarantulas are now becoming harder to find and the species is regarded as "lower risk" and "near-threatened". This means there is no conservation program in place to maintain numbers, but that they are close to being classed as "vulnerable".

SMUGGLED SPIDER
The red-kneed tarantula is strikingly patterned and has been a favorite with collectors. Although exporting the spiders is now banned, smugglers have been caught trying to take them out of their native countries.

HORSESHOE CRAB

Limulus polyphemus
Family: LIMULIDAE
Order: MEROSTOMATA

STATUS: Lower Risk (IUCN); not listed by CITES. Population unknown. There are 3 other marine invertebrates, regarded as related endangered species, that share the common name horseshoe crab: *Carcinoscorpius rotundicorunda*; *Tachyplcus gigas*, and *T. tridentatus*.

DISTRIBUTION: Sandy or muddy shores and shallow water in bays and estuaries of India, Indonesia, Malaysia, Philippines, Singapore, Thailand, Taiwan, and Vietnam; Atlantic coasts of Canada, U.S., and Mexico.

SIZE: Length: up to 2ft (60cm). Weight: adults 4lb (1.8kg).

FORM: A fossillike, armored invertebrate with a noticeable tail. The domed carapace (hard shell) carries a pair of compound eyes at its side and a smaller pair of simple eyes nearer the midline. The triangular abdomen bears a pointed tail spine that stabilizes the crab.

DIET: Small bivalves, worms, and other invertebrates; seaweed.

BREEDING: The male clasps the tail of the female and is towed around by her. Female digs shallow pit on midshore and lays 200–300 eggs; male sheds sperm over them. Larvae, known as trilobite larvae (because they resemble the fossil trilobites) emerge. Several larval stages are marked by molts. Maturity is reached after 16 molts and at about 10 years.

CONSERVATION: The future of the strange-looking horseshoe crab is a cause for concern among conservationists. For many years the animals were regarded as a common sight on the shore and in the shallow water of their native seas. However, when they come ashore to breed, they become vulnerable to disturbance by people. Like other bottom-dwelling marine arthropods, horseshoe crabs are easily caught.

CAUSE FOR CONCERN
Horseshoe crabs congregate at the edge of the tide and are easy to catch. Their numbers have been depleted by catching for use as farm food and fertilizer. They can swim on their backs using gill flaps, but they also plow through sand or mud, arching their bodies and pushing with their tail spine.

In Asia they are collected for food by local people. However, while they have been used in the souvenir trade, it is their collection for industrial use, such as for making chicken food and fertilizer, that seems to have most seriously affected their numbers. Given that fossils of these creatures have been found dating back to the time of dinosaurs, their value to our biodiversity is priceless.

GLOSSARY

ADAPTATION features of an animal that adjust it to its environment; may be produced by evolution, e.g., camouflage coloration.

ADULT a fully grown sexually mature animal; bird in final plumage.

ALGAE primitive plants ranging from microscopic to seaweeds, but lacking proper roots or leaves.

ALPINE living in mountainous areas, over 5,000 ft (1,500 m).

AMPHIBIOUS able to live both on land and in water.

ARACHNID one of a group of arthropods of the class Arachnida, characterized by simple eyes and four pairs of legs. Includes spiders and scorpions.

ARBOREAL living in trees.

ARTHROPOD the largest grouping in the animal kingdom having a hard, jointed exoskeleton and paired jointed legs. Includes insects, spiders, crabs, etc.

BILL often called the beak: the jaws of a bird, consisting of two bony mandibles, upper and lower, and their horny sheaths.

BIODIVERSITY the variety of species and the variation within them.

BIOME a major world landscape characterized by having similar plants and animals living in it, e.g., desert, jungle, forest.

BIPED any animal that walks on two legs. See quadruped.

BREEDING SEASON the entire cycle of reproductive activity, from courtship, pair formation (and often establishment of territory) through nesting to independence of young.

CAGE BIRD a bird kept in captivity; in this book it usually refers to birds taken from the wild.

CANOPY continuous (closed) or broken (open) layer in forests produced by the intermingling of branches of trees.

CARNIVORE meat-eating animal.

CARRION the flesh of dead animals.

CHRYSALIS the pupa in moths and butterflies.

CLASS a large group of related animals. Mammals, insects, and reptiles are all classes of animals.

CLOUD FOREST moist, high-altitude forest characterized by a dense understory and an abundance of ferns, mosses, and other plants growing on the trunks and branches of trees.

CONIFEROUS FOREST evergreen forests found in northern regions and mountainous areas, dominated by pines, spruce, and cedars.

CRUSTACEAN member of a class within the phylum Arthropoda typified by five pairs of legs, two pairs of antennae, a joined head and thorax, and calcereous deposits in the exoskeleton, e.g., crabs.

DECIDUOUS FOREST dominated by trees that lose their leaves in winter (or in the dry season).

DEFORESTATION the process of cutting down and removing trees for timber or to create open space for growing crops, grazing animals.

DESERT area of low rainfall typically with sparse scrub or grassland vegetation or lacking it altogether.

DISPERSAL the scattering of young animals going to live away from where they were born and brought up.

DIURNAL active during the day.

DOMESTICATION process of taming and breeding animals to provide help and useful products for humans.

ECOLOGY the study of plants and animals in relation to one another and to their surroundings.

ECOSYSTEM a whole system in which plants, animals, and their environment interact.

ENDEMIC found only in one geographical area, nowhere else.

EXTINCTION process of dying out of a species at the end of which the very last individual dies, and the species is lost forever.

FAMILY a group of closely related species that often also look quite similar. Zoological family names always end in -idae. Also used to describe a social group within a species comprising parents and their offspring.

GENUS (genera, pl.) a group of closely related species.

GESTATION the period of pregnancy in mammals, between fertilization of the egg and birth of the baby.

GILL respiratory organ that absorbs oxygen from the water. External gills occur in tadpoles. Internal gills occur in most fish.

HEN any female bird.

HERBIVORE an animal that eats plants by grazing as well as browsing.

HIBERNATION becoming inactive in winter, with lowered body temperature to save energy.

INCUBATION the act of keeping the egg or eggs warm or the period from the laying of eggs to hatching.

INDIGENOUS living naturally in a region; native (i.e. not an introduced species).

INSECT any air-breathing arthropod of the class Insecta, having a body divided into head, thorax, and abdomen, three pairs of legs, and sometimes two pairs of wings.

INSECTIVORE animal that feeds on insects. Also used as a group name for hedgehogs, shrews, moles, etc.

INVERTEBRATES animals that have no backbone (or other bones) inside their body, e.g., mollusks, insects, jellyfish, crabs.

JUVENILE a young animal that has not yet reached breeding age.

LARVA an immature form of an animal that develops into an adult form through metamorphosis.

LIVEBEARER animal that gives birth to fully developed young (usually refers to reptiles or fish).

MAMMAL any animal of the class Mammalia – warm-blooded vertebrate having mammary glands in the female that produce milk with which it nurses its young. The class includes bats, primates, rodents, and whales.

MARINE living in the sea.

METAMORPHOSIS transformation of a larva into an adult.

MIGRATION movement from one place to another and back again; usually seasonal.

MONTANE a mountain environment.

NATURAL SELECTION the main process driving evolution in which animals and plants are challenged by natural effects (such as predators and bad weather), resulting in survival of the fittest.

NESTLING a young bird still in the nest and dependent on its parents.

NOCTURNAL active at night.

NOMADIC animals that have no fixed home, but wander continuously.

OMNIVORE an animal that eats a wide range of both animal and vegetable food.

ORDER a subdivision of a class of animals, consisting of a series of animal families.

ORGANISM any member of the animal or plant kingdom; a body that has life.

ORNITHOLOGIST zoologist specializing in the study of birds.

OVIPAROUS producing eggs that hatch outside the body of the mother (in fish, reptiles, birds, etc).

PARASITE an animal or plant that lives on or within the body of another (the host) from which it obtains nourishment. The host is often harmed by the association.

PASSERINE any bird of the order Passeriformes; includes songbirds.

PELAGIC living in the upper waters of the open sea or large lakes.

PHYLUM zoological term for a major grouping of animal classes. The whole animal kingdom is divided into about 30 phyla, of which the vertebrates form part of just one.

PLANKTON minute animals and plants drifting in open water.

PLUMAGE the covering of feathers on a bird's body.

POPULATION a distinct group of animals of the same species or all the animals of that species.

PREDATOR an animal that kills live prey.

PREHENSILE capable of grasping.

PRIMARY FOREST forest that has always been forest and has not been cut down and regrown at some time.

PRIMATES a group of mammals that includes monkeys and apes.

QUADRUPED any animal that walks on four legs.

RANGE the total geographical area over which a species is distributed.

REPTILE any member of the cold-blooded class Reptilia, such as crocodiles, lizards, snakes, with external covering of scales or horny plates.

SAVANNA open grasslands with scattered trees and low rainfall, usually in warm areas.

SCRUB vegetation dominated by shrubs (woody plants usually with more than one stem).

SLASH-AND-BURN AGRICULTURE method of farming in which the unwanted vegetation is cleared by cutting down and burning.

SPAWNING the laying and fertilizing of eggs by fish, amphibians etc.

STEPPE open grassland in parts of the world where the climate is too harsh for trees to grow.

SUBSPECIES a subpopulation of a single species whose members are similar to each other but differ from the typical form for that species; often called a race.

TAXONOMY the branch of biology concerned with classifying organisms into groups according to similarities in their structure, origins, or behavior. The main categories, in order of increasing broadness, are: species, genus, family, order, class, phylum.

TERRESTRIAL living on land.

TERRITORY defended space.

TUNDRA open grassy or shrub-covered lands of the far north.

VERTEBRATE animal with a backbone (e.g., fish, mammal, reptile), usually with skeleton made of bones, but sometimes softer cartilage.

VIVIPAROUS (of most mammals and a few other vertebrates) giving birth to active young – not laying eggs.

ZOOLOGIST person who studies animals. (Zoology is the study of animals).

INDEX

Tienes